THE
RENAISSANCE
MISSIONARY

The Renaissance Missionary

The Faith Adventures of Glenn Elliot Hickey

Daniel Glenn Hickey

Daniel Hickey
recifedaniel@gmail.com

ISBN: 978-1-7337964-4-6

Illustrations: Sara Senseman Mack
    artistcouple.com

Book design: H. K. Stewart

Library of Congress copyright registration number: TXu002190899

Printed in the United States of America

This book is printed on archival-quality paper that meets
requirements of the American National Standard for Information
Sciences, Permanence of Paper, Printed Library Materials, ANSI
Z39.48-1984.

To my partner and amor **Maria Sousa**, *who has been the water and sunshine that persisted until this book was ready to bloom.*

To my **Aunt Glenna Lybrand**, *who knew my dad as only a wise sister can, and whose uncommon inspiration, faith and humor remain a constant grace to our family.*

Contents

FOREWORD

"You really never know your parents like their friends do."

— Dolly Parton

If I had known the challenges of trying to accurately interpret my parent's life when I had this idea seven years ago, I would have never tried it. Over time the dream of telling this story grew into a life of its own, so I just learned to serve and celebrate it. By the grace of God and so many others we were able to complete this journey.

Dr. Ray Granade, Professor of History and Director of Library Services at Ouachita Baptist University, said before he had even seen the manuscript that "the main problem with this book is that you wrote it."

Time bore him out in discovering the truth of the Apostle Paul in 1 Corinthians, 13:12. "For now we see (our parents) through a glass, darkly; but then face to face: now I know in part; but then shall I know even as also I am known." The immense gift of this work was discovering through the eyes of their contemporaries just how luminous they were in the darkness.

Introduction

"Dr. Hickey is an outstanding representative of those who give their lives in service…one who is dreaming the impossible dream and coupling it with good common sense…a catalyst of fellowship among churches on mission together."

Dr. Daniel R. Grant,
President of Ouachita Baptist University,
when recognizing Dr. Glenn Hickey as
"Director of Missions of the Year" on February 26, 1987

My father, Dr. Glenn Hickey, was an original, a nerdy head, language freak missionary who loved to sing barbershop, ham radio his friends around the world, and ride his bike to infinity. His life was about preaching and teaching biblical Greek and the Christian life way in Brazilian Portuguese and Arkansas slang. He was a boy from Mount Ida, Arkansas, who fulfilled his destiny in many cultures and places by making life a series of spiritual adventures.

GLENN ELLIOT AND GLENNA LOU

The Hickeys of Mount Ida, Arkansas walked by the light of a strange north star of family, hard work, Christian mysticism, and the fervent pursuit of the dreams available to them. They blew themselves along by the fuel of stubborn optimism that kept emerging as surely as the dogwood flowers in the Ouachita Mountains each spring.

Both Glenn Elliot and Glenna Lou Hickey displayed a noble serenity in their telling of being born at home in Oden, Arkansas. Their parents, Glenn and Lula Hickey, set themselves up to flourish in the commerce and culture of rural Arkansas. My Grandfather Glenn was assiduously taught the no-shortcut, hard-driving mercantile life by his father, Sam, in the general store in Oden, Arkansas. My Grandmother Lula combined an astonishing skill set of social intelligence, musical talent, and the homemaking arts. Passionate about music, she started her own kitchen band as a teenager with the flair of a 1920 flapper. Homemaking at that time was creating life in quilts, preserving strawberries, healing cuts and hurts, attending church activities every Sunday, tending a farm, and making life fun for her children in the frugality of the 1930s. The soft-spoken giant of the Hickey family system, she labored to soften the Protestant work-ethic abuses of her husband upon the kids.

My Aunt Glenna offers the best possible contemplation of the Hickey story. "We lived in a rock house on a farm. We had gardens, orchards, chickens, and cattle. One of the things I remember is having to come home from school every afternoon when Glenn and I went up in the loft of our barn to shuck corn to feed the chickens. I suppose the chickens were hungry, but I thought that was a hard job. We had an outhouse. We had well water, which was inside the back porch. The back porch was full of curing hams hanging down. Dad would kill hogs, hang them on the back porch, and smoke them. I loved that smoked ham before it was cooked. I would cut pieces of ham off when Mother and Dad were not watching. I think Glenn

Glenn Elliot, his sister Glenna Lou and cousins. Back row: Martha Pierce holding Charlotte Hickey; middle row: Betty Pierce, holding Mary Gayle Pierce, Glenna Lou and Glenn Elliot Hickey; front row: Linda Pierce and Mary Elizabeth Hickey.

did the same thing. They would say 'don't eat that ham, you'll get worms,' but that didn't stop us.

"My grandparents, Sam and Lizzie Hickey, also lived in Oden, probably a half mile from our house. Sam was pretty much all business, and he didn't have a lot to say, but my grandmother was a quite talkative and lively lady. This was true not only in her relationship with other people but also in her church life. She was a Baptist but went to every revival no matter the denomination, and she was a Baptist shouter. She shouted during the sermon when something moved her. One time, they came to visit us at First Baptist Mount Ida, and we had a young pastor at that time. And I don't know if it was during the song, during the sermon, or what but Grandma stood up and shouted—a good loud shout and 'praise the Lord!' She raised her hands, and the pastor just said, 'let us pray.' So, when in doubt, pray!

"Grandpa Hickey and my dad, Glenn, had a general store in Oden. They sold groceries, clothing, and farm supplies. I remember they had big fifty-five-gallon wooden barrels with the metal strips around them. They bought crackers and dried coconut. Imagine in Oden, Arkansas how long a barrel of sweet dried coconut might last, but I remember as a child I heaved myself up on the top of that barrel to about my waistline and reached down in there to get a handful of coconut to eat. They also had loads of candy at the store but that didn't mean we got any.

"In 1945, when there was a fire at the Oden Store, Sam Hickey and Glenn moved the store to Mount Ida. I met a woman at the nursing home the other day who knew the Lybrands and the Hickeys. After we introduced ourselves as Bob and Glenna Lybrand, she lit up. 'Lybrand! Oh, I know all those Lybrands! Oh, they were the best musicians,' and started naming off the family musicians. She paused and asked Bob, 'What's your name?' 'I'm Bob.' 'Oh, you play the fiddle and sing. I remember that!'"

Bob Lybrand grew up in a large Mount Ida clan and married my Aunt Glenna Lou in 1954. Every Saturday for a summer, Bob played the fiddle in a band called the Arkansas Playboys in Mena. Featured on the radio for thirty minutes weekly, they were very happy to make enough money for everybody to go to a restaurant and have hamburger steaks.

Glenna continued, "Since she remembered the Lybrand family so well, I said to her, 'Well did you ever buy anything at Hickey Hardware?'

"'Hickey Hardware! Why sure I did! I bought a bunch of stuff there. When that Glenn Hickey moved into here, this town came alive! Until him, everything was just as dead as it could be. We had Elder's store over there and Sim's store and so on, but, boy, he came in here and really opened this place up.'" (Glenn Hickey, my grandfather, was the first to introduce modern appliances such as washing machines and refrigerators to that part of Montgomery County.)

"Our other side grandparents, James and Amanda Liles, lived at Big Fork, Arkansas. He was a Baptist minister, and during that time there were a lot of little churches around who had no minister, and he was a circuit rider. One of my pastors knew him said he would ride eighteen miles on his mule on Sundays to preach. Glenn and I we always went to church. Dad was a deacon, and mom taught what we call Juniors Sunday School class [preteens]. She shared that Sunday school class with Ann Sparks, Layne Spark's mother. Both of us were converted[1] in childhood and baptized in a creek. I remember the revival meetings because they always lasted two weeks, and Mother always hosted the visiting preachers, so she should be rewarded for that." (Bob and Glenna Lybrand, Interview, October 2017)

Glenn and Glenna were never close growing up. Glenn enjoyed his privileged position as the first-born son, and this inspired his little sister's antipathy. Only adulthood allowed an enduring mutual admiration to enter the picture. The memories were woven in deeply for Glenna, "Glenn was three years older and constantly finding new ways to be embarrassed by my presence. When we were little, he walked ten feet ahead of me to avoid any public association. As a teenager, he was very diplomatic and would always say the right thing, while I would always blurt out exactly what I was thinking."

Glenn's embarrassment did not stop Glenna, who was elected the president of the Arkansas/Missouri Beta club (Beta Club is a national organization founded to promote the ideals of academic achievement, character, leadership, and service among elementary and secondary school students) held at the Lafayette Hotel in Little Rock in March of 1951. Glenna followed her brother all the way to Ouachita Baptist

College (O.B.C.) where her star rose in Theater and Speech. Thankfully for Glenna, he got married off and graduated one year after her arrival, leaving the college in her hands. Glenna had a great time, frequently attending the black gospel church in town where she was warmly welcomed. By now she was a pioneering and self-possessed co-ed, pulling off such stunts such as organizing a campus wide "bunny hop" dance in the student union on a sacred Wednesday church night, breaking a Baptist campus rule, and setting up a life course that broke the mold.

The Gang of Four

My grandfather Glenn was the oldest of four siblings, Harold, Bernice and Sammy. My great aunt Bernice married Carol Pierce, and they had my father's first cousins Betty, Martha, Mary Gayle and Linda Pierce. Aside from having to learn how to deal with his outspoken sister Glenna, Dad had the opportunity to learn from girl cousins Martha and Betty Pierce who thought higher of him. Daughters of next-door neighbors Uncle Carol and Aunt Bernice Pierce, they forged a gang of four who played endless games in the ravine and creek between the homes. Martha recalled, "Every time we got together was a good time. Glenn was one year older and like a brother to me. I looked out for him, and he looked out for me. We could take an old rubber tire and roll it forever or make a stick and a can work for our entertainment." (Martha Pierce, Interview, 2018)

We had summers of crawdads, fireflies, and enchanting trips to the Charlton swimming hole, the "coldest water in America" according to Betty Pierce (Sparks). One summer outing Glenn noticed the dam was mossy and slimy enough to attempt a risky slide down into the frigid waters. His slide did not end well, since he overestimated the slime. He was laid up the rest of the day with a skinned backside. In winters, they chased the chill away with indoor creativity and improvisation, taking breaks to warm up by the potbellied stove. "I remember in the winter we would cut all the pictures out of the [Sears and Montgomery Ward's] catalogues and line them around the rooms for endless fun." (Betty Pierce Sparks, Interview, 2017)

Glenn Elliot "Whizzing" into the Mount Ida square.

The Mount Ida Dreamer

The image of a freckled-faced dark-haired thirteen-year old boy "whizzing" down Highway 270 into the Mount Ida square on his motorized homebuilt bike in 1944 betrays the blessing of being part of a generation of American dreamers too young for war.

Dad later considered his ten-year-old dreamer life. "Dreams die when they are neglected, when they are not relived, revisited, and celebrated with regularity. One of my earliest and most vivid memories as a ten-year-old boy was the dream to own a whizzer motorbike and ride it up the road from Oden to Pine Ridge or maybe even to Highway 270 and the paved road to Mount Ida. A *whizzer* was a motorized kit that could be installed on an ordinary bicycle. I already had the bicycle. The kit costs seventy-five dollars, which according to my dad was a big problem. (Really his problem was with the idea of a ten-year old turned loose on a machine that could go up to 40 miles an hour!) I was thirteen before I got my motorbike. Three years is a long time for to wait. It's was one third of my lifetime! Do you know how I kept that dream alive? *Mechanix Illustrated* magazine sold it by direct ads. Every month when it came in the mail, I would first look for the ad with the boy racing down the road, seeing myself someday as the proud owner of this dream bike.

"Churches exist to enable people to re-visit and celebrate their highest and noblest dreams and aspirations. True worship enables us to do just that. Our hearts are lifted up in celebration and praise, our souls are stirred, and our life dreams are re-kindled within us. We look momentarily not at a picture in a magazine but into the very face of God as Isaiah did in the temple."[2]

Big Fork Reunions

Oden and Mount Ida are in the middle of Ouachita National Forest, so Dad was given primeval magic and solitude while being part of a jovial tribe far from the noise and rush of city life. Montgomery County is one of the whitest counties in Arkansas. Dad and Glenna's early formation did not include racial diversity, and yet they both as adults emanated an intense curiosity, backed up by choices to be close to people from different ethnicities and cultures.

Yummy food gatherings nurtured a sense of self beyond the nuclear Hickeys. The simple abundance of aromas cascaded from the tables into their collective soul.

Dad could still smell the rolls, "Some of the most precious memories of my childhood are of those family reunions. The Hickey family wasn't much on reunions, but my maternal grandmother was from a family with a long and sacred history of family reunions, and every four years was the Smith/Liles family reunion at Big Fork, Arkansas at the blue hole on Cates Creek. There was the finest swimming hole in the county with crystal-clear water and a twenty-foot bank for diving. There was a gigantic gravel bar under towering cottonwood trees with plenty of room to park the wagons and log trucks that would come out of those hills for the reunion. They carried some benches out of the nearby Baptist church where my grandfather preached and turned them facing each other, and began to spread the feast: fried chicken, chicken and dumplings, homemade rolls, and banana pudding the likes of which you have never seen in all your life. What a reunion that no one wanted to miss! There won't be anybody missing from the great reunion of the family of God. Everybody who belongs there will be there because God himself through his ministering angels will gather us in. What a great and glorious gathering that will be!"[3]

How Things Work

Dad was eternally curious and always on the vanguard of high tech. His theo-techno mind loved to explore what could be possible for expanding the Christian life.

"In my early childhood, I was always fascinated by the way things work. At eight years of age, I figured out how to remove the hand-cranked generator from an old-fashioned discarded wall telephone and give my sister and cousins some shocking surprises when they placed their hand in a tub of water or reached for some wired object. Quite early in my life, my curiosity for the way things work paid off for the Hickey General Mercantile Store in Oden, Arkansas. We were among the first families in Arkansas to install *Servel* kerosene refrigerators. My dad was soon selling them to mountain people all over western Arkansas. I was curious about this machine and the mystery of making ice from fire. I studied the maintenance manual and learned how to clean the wick periodically, replace the thermal safety link if needed, and unstop the kerosene line when it clogged up. By age nine, I was riding the Oden mail routes on weekends and summers doing the routine maintenance for *Servel* customers. Many folks were deathly afraid of touching anything inside this strange, newfangled machine for fear it would blow up. Childhood curiosity and fascination with new things plunged in where adult fear of the new and unfamiliar dared not tread."

"Jesus said, 'Unless you shall become as little children, you shall in no wise enter the kingdom of heaven.' He was speaking of humility, trust, and obedience. Maybe there is yet another way. He calls us to become children again in a changing world. Along with childlike faith, we Christians need childlike curiosity, a hunger for knowledge about our world, how people think and live."[4]

The Prankster's Rites of Passage

Sixty-three years later, Dad reflected publicly on his early gratifying mischievous activity. "He was a small-town lad, son of two generations of country merchants and farmers. He was the runt of his class. He couldn't play basketball because he was a short, asthmatic child. Some said he was a smart kid but quite mischievous. I guess that was because, if you didn't play basketball, you had to do something to get attention."[5]

Layne Sparks was Dad's closest buddy, practically family since he joined the original gang of four Pierce/Hickey children who were all neighbors in Oden. He later married Glenn and Glenna's cousin Betty Pierce. Dad first distinguished himself as prankster with the genius idea to put sulfur in the large potbellied stove in the one-room schoolhouse on a Sunday evening. When the janitor lit the fire early the next morning, he was astonished, and school was immediately closed that day. The boys were emboldened by their capacities and quickly designed the next stunt. The music teacher was Miss Odessa Holt, and most boys didn't like music. Layne enjoyed the memory: "Miss Odessa was an old maid, and on Halloween night, we jacked her car up, put some wood underneath it, and when she started the car the wheels spun out. She tried again and again. Finally, she got out, looked back and just smiled, then laughed out loud and got a big kick out of it."

Wayne Lanier joined Layne and Dad for the most dangerous feat to date. They had to hoist their heavy homemade propaganda sign to the roof of school, of which Dick Douglass was the principal. It required upside-down nailing and tying ropes over the edge of a steep roof in the dark with a thirty-foot drop to the hard limestone sidewalk. Since it took several days to find someone to take it down, all the students silently enjoyed the spectacle of the newly named *The Dick Douglass Death House*. (Source Layne and Betty Pierce Sparks, Interview, Jan 2018)

Dad enjoyed preaching on his first smoking experience. "When I was about 10 years old, I had a good friend by the name of Maurice Mullenix. My dad and grandad had a country store in Oden, Arkansas. His dad had a small store just across the street. In those days, almost everyone smoked cigarettes. We thought we needed to 'grow up' and start smoking. We decided on a plan. We would steal a pack of cigarettes from his dad's store. We'd slip away and smoke 'em and then the next time we'd steal a pack from my dad's store. Maurice stole his pack, and we went down under the bridge where Lick Creek flows into the Ouachita River and smoked our first cigarettes.

"I don't know to this day how my dad found out about our plan, but the next morning we were out in the barn. "'Son, when you finish shucking the corn and I finish milking the cows, I want to talk to you.' I knew something bad was coming. When we met, he said, 'Now son, I know you and Maurice swiped some cigarettes from somewhere and went down the road and smoked 'em. Now if you are going to take up smoking, I want you to know, you are going to have to pay for those cigarettes yourself. You'd better not ever steal anything from my store. So, if you are going to smoke, get you a job somewhere and go to work to pay for your smoking habit because I'm not going to pay for it.'

"Do you know that was about the last cigarette I ever smoked? My dad challenged me. He dared me to have the courage to be honest and consistent in my life. Jesus is that kind of friend to us. He said to his disciples, 'Launch into the deep waters.' Arise to the challenge of your discipleship."[6]

By age sixteen, Dad's best bud was Hugh Demby. With zealous encouragement from my Grandfather Glenn, they embarked on what he expected would an epic boys-to-men float trip on the wild and vanishing Ouachita River before it became Lake Ouachita. Hugh recollected, "We didn't do too well fishing, but thunderstorms were moving in, and I said we better get off the river. We found an old barn, got our sleeping bags, and stretched them out on the hay. Back in them days, all those barns were full of copperheads, so we didn't sleep a wink, sat up all night scared to death that the snakes were gonna get us. We got up and were getting ready to shove off. Now, this was close to a road crossing and before we got back in the water Glenn Sr. showed up. We were never so glad to get picked up!" (Hugh Demby, Interview, May 2015)

Into joyful reminiscing, Hugh could not help but unload another story: "Glenn was quiet, always real sharp in the books, and a very nice, gentlemanly person. You could almost predict that he was going to be somebody important in life.

One of the things I always think about was after his dad bought the first Hydrostatic [automatic] Oldsmobile that came out in 1948. At that time hardly anybody had a car. After school, we would all load up, and Glenn Elliot would take us around. Glenn's father thought he was always taking good care of his car, which I assume he meant to.

One evening he took us all up to Mount Ida Mountain, and it was the closest I ever come to getting killed in a car. We got up there in this brand new Olds, and Glenn wound her up and let it go. We came off the top and we started down through there, and he saw it was getting out of control. Now, in a standard car you gear[shift] down, and it helped to slow down, but this was a Hydrostatic, new to everybody including Glenn Elliot. So, then he reached up just by instinct, and pulled it into reverse. When that rubber quit burning, and all the smoke cleared out, we crawled up off the floorboard, and we thought he had ruined the car. He got it started back up. We were still scared to death, but it ran well, and he brought it on home and never said anything to anybody about it." (Hugh Demby, Interview, May, 2015)

Persistence as Taught by Glenn and Glenna's Father

Dad's father, Glenn, the businessman, worked with such persistence that even at play he could not relax if there was something to achieve. The family fondly remembers this all too clearly on a summer vacation day on Lake Ouachita when Glenn Elliot and Glenna were young adults and he decided to learn how to water ski in front of everybody. Layne Sparks got him ready, and the boat accelerated to the decisive moment. Glenn emerged briefly only to sink deeper, with everybody yelling, "Let go of the rope." He refused to let go of the rope. He believed eventually he would rise if persistent. Gasps of relief when he did let go and floated back up, gasping for air, only to insist on another round, then another, each time breaking his previous record for underwater ski time. He never made it on top of the water that day, but persevered stubbornly in his folly, intensely entertaining those who knew him well. That story was always retold, and particularly relished by my dad and Aunt Glenna. (Glenna and Bob Lybrand, Interview, October 2017)

Travelitis

Both my dad and Aunt Glenna shared an early itch to travel, always eager to risk and reach out of their safe Mount Ida haven for the discoveries and serendipities that rewarded them in new places and cultures. Glenna made it out of the country first, joining Bob on his U.S. Army assignment to post-war Germany. She braved the radical culture change, the German language, the odorous German cheeses, and the spartan apartment they shared with another couple. This only fueled her wanderlust. While holding down the school librarian job in Mount Ida, she crowned her "the places you will go" bucket list by becoming a mega-mile global trekker. In course of her travels she never went alone, but always involved friends and family. She sailed all the seas and toured all the continents, including

Antarctica. Crossing borders into 87 countries, she created hundreds of stories and new friendships in villages across the globe.

"She loved anything that was out of the ordinary, we did a lot of adventure travel. Sometimes she just had to make me go…Vietnam, Tibet, Indonesia, Antarctica, on and on…and she so loved the people." (Friend Betty Prince, who accompanied her to 55 countries and 7 continents, Interview, 2019)

If there was ever a family competition for travel miles and adventures, Aunt Glenna left my dad in the dust long before he even made it out of Arkansas!

The Brotherhood of Four

They were four young friends with some talent and lots of opportunities to be center stage. What could be sweeter for young men in 1949? Zahle Elms, Henry Wood, David Moore, and Glenn Hickey sang together for the next forty-four years, enjoying a rare blend of personalities and melodies, and with enough stories, pranks, and fights to write a Netflix series.

Zahle journaled zealously on the quartet's story:

> We were freshmen together in the fall of 1949. Glenn made a big enough impression on me. He had heard of a trio I was part of and already had thought of how to improve it: 'What you guys really need is a bass. I just worked a church camp with a tremendous bass, a guy named Henry Wood, or 'Woody.' As time worked things out, Woody joined and later the baritone bowed out. Glenn said, 'I read music and I think I can do it.' He worked out tremendously! Another guy bowed out, and we came up with David Moore, and that was the beginning.
>
> We were together 1949-53, and we drew on each other and practiced a lot. Glenn had played saxophone in high school, and Woody played the trombone, and he also read music. David Moore was a music major, so by the spring semester of our freshman year we had

settled on who was in the quartet. We began to build our repertoire, singing at parties and vespers services, which usually happened every day, being a religious college. So, by the end of the first year, our interest increased. We had begun to take it very seriously. Of course, you needed the range of a bass and a tenor, but the most difficult part to find and sing is a good baritone. That's what Glenn had, a good ear. We were very lucky to have Glenn as a baritone in our quartet.[7]

Woody was a recipient of Glenn's idea of fun in those days. "I first met Glenn in the summer of '49 at Siloam Springs, and we started singing together. Glenn was friends with this fellow from Hot Springs named Steven Austin. I was naive at the time, but Glenn and Austin made a deal with a young woman, and introduced me to Priscilla Pukelwart, and we went on a couple of dates. It was only two years later that I saw her again at Ouachita Baptist College (O.B.C.)[8] and found out: 'My name is Helen Overton!'" (Henry Wood Interview, 2015)

Once David and Woody got into a disagreement over song selection: "David made a wisecrack about my choice of a song, so I shoved him up against a wall. 'Why you Sad Sack!' [A blundering, inept person … a sad sack is so unlucky in love that when his girlfriend splits, his family sides with her—Merriam Webster[9]] and he took a big swing at me. By that time Glenn and Zahle had gotten between us, but Glenn got the lick and cracked his nose," Woody said. (Henry Wood Interview, 2015)

Zahle Elms recalls an attack of the funny bones. "On Tiger Day for prospective students at O.B.C. we sang for the dedication of Conger Hall. We ended with the Dry Bones story in song out of the book of Ezekiel in Old Testament. This has syncopation, and there's is a tendency to get faster and faster. David Moore reached around and grabbed Glenn's coat, whose responsibility it was to go faster and faster. He tried to slow Glenn's rhythm and beat down. We got three fourths finished, and all burst out in laughter, and never did get the Ezekiel's bones connected."[10]

Zahle and Woody cherished the camera salvation story. "The quartet was on a return trip from Jeff City, Missouri, and stopped for

The Ouachita Baptist College Quartet: Zahle Elms, Henry Wood, Glenn Hickey, (left to right) and David Moore (standing).

a short break on a scenic overlook close to Eureka Springs. Now, Glenn was always meticulous and wanted to do things right, and he had received an Argosy 3 camera as a graduation gift and was a zealous steward, but this afternoon got distracted. Later, seventy-five miles down the road, an "Oh shit," or something like that screeched up from the back seat. Rarely out of his zone of tranquility, Glenn was so distraught that the group drove back the seventy-five miles to find it gone, most likely forever. It was a week later that he received box with the following explanation inside. 'Dear Mr. Hickey, we found your camera, we want to return it to you.' There was much rejoicing in the group, and it was indeed a spiritual experience for Glenn that restored his faith in humanity." (Zahle Elms and Henry Wood, Interviews)

Zahle Elms' narration of the quartet's story reveals the magical age between forever young and wisdom they were passing. They settled forever the question of socialism:

On route between concerts from Springfield, Missouri to Little Rock, Arkansas, we got into a terrific argument about socialism, and it got to be a shouting match. We wore our voices out on that drive. It wasn't about socialism, not in political sense. It was about poor people who we knew personally in the state of Arkansas. It had to do with black people, how they were treated, how to get to responsible, moral socialism, and what we should be doing to overcome the wide disparagement between very poor people and people who were much better off. It was about how to treat people, what kind of programs, what did we morally owe to poor people. We felt superior because we were all in college, and college was a little bit more exclusive sixty years ago. There was a feeling that if you helped people too much, they would stop working and start looking for handouts.

As Christians what should we be doing, regardless of what we thought some freeloader was doing to take advantage of the situation? How do you go and try to do the right thing? Everybody was trying to prove their points based on their own personal experience, like: We didn't have much but got along well and made it work without handouts. You just can't prove your point like that. It's not about you. It's about classes of people. It was all good discussion, and not like we would get mad at each other, but sometimes we got loud. Politics didn't have anything to do with it. Being from a Christian college, and as religious beings ourselves, our point of reference was always what was the right thing to do as a Christian. If you pay attention, you know there are Christians who think widely on this particular subject, all being convinced they are doing the right thing.

But to speak specifically of Glenn's contribution to our four-cornered friendship, he occupied a rather special place, in that David was more carefree, and Woody was very serious (high priest of the group). He kept us all in line. Glenn, we called the 'professor,' since he was far and away the best student of the four. He was a good preacher, well prepared and used scriptures well. We admired his academic capacity and how he handled the complexities of an inflected language like Greek. He never varied from his stated goal, from when the first time we talked in college, was that he wanted to be a missionary. I remember him telling me that was the reason he came to Ouachita. And of course, that's what he did. He never wavered. All of us stumbled around. Even after we finished our four-year college careers together, I was well aware that Glenn and Dorothy were always preparing themselves as a couple to go on the mission field.

So, what did the Ouachita Experience mean? For me it was the personal relationships formed there, above all ours in the quartet, which was being accepted completely in a small tightly knit group where it was impossible to offend or permanently alienate each other. David and Henry had a fight; we kicked David out of the group; I once bit Hickey's finger so hard it almost dislodged an incisor. Being separated for years seems to have no effect on anything. Thirty seconds after we get together, it's as if nothing ever changed. I've always thought we are closer than brothers. One doesn't choose one's brother, but we choose each other as friends in spite of our numerous short comings and faults. I was whiny and nit-picking, Woody was cheap and watched his money, David was optimistic to a fault and had a temper, and Hickey, yeah, Hickey was smarter than the rest of us, but we forgave him. Other than that, we were perfect. 1993 was our last time together. (Zahle Elms Journals)[11]

DOROTHY THOMERSON

My mother, Dorothy Thomerson, or "Dot" was the joy of Third Baptist Malvern, Arkansas and was playing piano for the choir and congregation by age fourteen. She figured out early in life to lean in on her gifts and seize the day. She took over the choir at age sixteen and assumed more home duties than her peers because her mother, Amanda, had diabetes. Born in Malvern, Arkansas, she was the youngest of six brothers and sisters, Florence, Roy, Eva, Coy and Alton. She lost two brothers early. Alton died in childbirth, and Coy died in a gun accident after returning from WW II.

Dorothy's niece Martha (Martha and Larry Thomerson, children of Roy and Louise Thomerson) reflects on the Thomerson home where her father, Roy, and Dorothy were formed: "I remember going to Malvern to visit Grandma Thomerson. She lived in a white house with a short fence out front and right across the road were the railroad tracks. The house would shake when the trains went by. My favorite thing about going to Grandma's house was the old piano when you first walked in. Even though it was out of tune, Grandma could work magic, and all by ear." (Martha Thomas reflections, 2018) This piano, and my Grandmother Amanda's passion for it, was the greatest gift imaginable to my mom's childhood.

Mom always included three qualities that defined her family: poor, hardworking, and very Southern Baptist. Homer Patrick Thomerson, her dad, worked very hard at the Malvern ACME brick factory for his whole career. As she was preparing for Ouachita Baptist College, Mom discovered his body in the outhouse on December 29, 1948, when she was eighteen. Her church community rallied passionately to her side, funding her college education, and always cheering her piano, choir, and worship leadership when she came home.

"Dorothy would still come back on Sundays to lead the music at church from the piano. I remember our congregation would call out any number from the hymnal and she would immediately begin playing it." (Arkie Neal Remley, Interview, 2019) "Amanda, Dorothy's mother, never missed a Sunday singing in the choir for as far back as I can remember." (Bill Golding, Dorothy's Cousin, Interview, 2019)

"My parents, Roy and Louise Thomerson, moved to Gurdon, Arkansas after my daddy finished pharmacy school in 1950. Daddy bought out a local drugstore. Over the next thirty-nine years they worked very hard getting their store going and thriving." (Martha Thomas reflections, 2018)

Mom was a big fan of Uncle Roy for two reasons. He was a heroic veteran of WW II, one of those who did not like attention. Later, she admired the decades of service to the Gurdon community he and Aunt Louise provided through the Thomerson Drug Store. The Hickey's would return on furloughs from Brazil, and Uncle Roy would order them to help themselves to anything in the Gurdon store that they needed for their return to the mission field. Mom and Dad would sheepishly gather up their favorite merchandise and valiantly offer to pay, to no avail. Uncle Roy and Aunt Louise also made sure I got a bar of my favorite American candy, absent on the mission field at that time, a Milky Way.

Dorothy already had admirers before Glenn came into the picture. "Dot and I had some things in common. She was the soprano soloist for the choir one year at Ouachita when we did Handle's *The Messiah*, and I was the tenor soloist that year. I remember and can hear her now singing 'I know that my redeemer liveth.' She did such a marvelous job on that aria. She handled the high notes very well. She was almost a couverture soprano. I would sit on the dais, (rostrum) waiting to do my solo, and would think, I don't really deserve to be on the same stage as her right now. She had such a beautiful voice." (Zahle Elms, Interview, 2016).

Dad was also in the O.B.C. choir. Mom got a mutual friend to ask him on her behalf to the Sadie Hawkins Hayride and sing along. (Sadie Hawkins was the rare yearly event when the women ask the men for a date) Dad agreed with glee. Turns out his imagination was already kindled. 'Her jet-black hair and charismatic stage presence delivering those stunning soprano arias was quite overwhelming!' This partnership born in the simplicity of the O.B.C. choir triumphed over fifty-eight years of cultural, physical, and spiritual adjustments to remain a light for their community and family.

Valedictorian of his Mount Ida graduating class of 1949, Dad went on to Ouachita Baptist College where he graduated in January of 1953. Along the way came the two most consequential events of his life—ordination to the Gospel Ministry on March 21, 1950 and his marriage to Dorothy Thomerson. Lucky for him, Mom was all in on this life of service to a higher calling. They started out with the simple mantra of surrendering to the call of God, and their music lightened the load along the way. They were married on September 3, 1952, and honeymooned on Petit Jean Mountain in Arkansas. After both graduating from O.B.C. the next year, Dad was accepted into

Southwestern Baptist Theological Seminary, and the couple dove headfirst into seminary and church culture.

Their imaginations were fired by dreams of foreign missions inspired by heroes like missionary Clyde Hankins, a self-supporting wild man who was entirely sold out to the cause of Jesus Christ in Brazil and beyond. He just happened to serve briefly as pastor of First Baptist Mount Ida. Always hawking his Brazilian frugal frontier missionary glamour, he intoxicated Mom and Dad with fresh roasted Brazilian coffee and stories of spiritually living on the edge.

The debonair couple already with foreign mission expectations, May 1951.

Many years later, Dad would praise Hankins for altering his life course: "The pastor was a missionary on extended furlough from Brazil, Clyde Hankins. On the last Sunday night before he was to return to Brazil, he preached a missionary sermon. God spoke to that fifteen-year-old and several others that night. It was much like I imagine Elijah's call was, sudden, unexpected, but unmistakable. 'I need you,' God seemed to say. 'Will you come with me? I'll not tell you now exactly what I want you to do, but I need you on my mission field.' Life was never the same after that call of God on my life, sixty-three years ago."[12]

It took Mom and Dad three pastorates and twelve years of marriage before they boarded the *Del Sud* Ocean Liner for Brazil in 1964.

The Dorothy & Glenn Duet Star Tour of Wellington, Texas

(The Preacher Boy Observations)

After stints at Eagle Mt. and Corinth Baptist Churches, Dad and Mom emerged as small-town stars at First Baptist Wellington, Texas. They inspired with their musical gifts and servant hearts. In later years, their faces always lit up when the names of Gary West, Randal Scott, Dickey Lindsey or Richard Carter came up. These were their original "Preacher Boy Disciples."

The following observations are Randal and Gary returning the favor: "They agreed to come to serve First Baptist Wellington only if salary terms were LOWERED, which impressed a lot of people. They only had one car, and Dorothy walked to the square to get her groceries, fussing with the store owners when they insisted on taking groceries home for her. Dorothy's talent was exceptional! I couldn't understand how she could do it. She played watching the choir director or the soloist with or without music" (Randal Scott, Interview, 2016).

"Glenn was very evangelistic, but never shouted or frothed at the mouth with it. He had a quiet, gentle spirit, and people just responded to that, and he treated people with all kinds of respect and dignity." (Gary West, Interview, 2016)

It was in the wide array of social and racial classes in the Texas panhandle that Dad began to practice openness to everyone who he reached out to. He used his status as the pastor of the largest church in town to reach the marginalized and the golf country clubbers. He enjoyed hearing their stories long before sharing his message.

"Glenn and Dorothy duets were often requested, especially for funerals. (The Funeral Director, member of the church, would call them) 'He Lifted Me' was a favorite, and Glenn and Dorothy also would linger and visit the family. Glenn's favorite verse during that time—he almost always ended his sermons with it, was Romans 12:1-2 'Be ye not conformed to this world.' (He used it so much that I thought, doesn't he know any other verses?) Glenn helped start a Hispanic mission in Wellington, was a master of the art of visitation, and was a pastoral counselor before it became popular." (Randal Scott, Interview, 2016)

Gary West was the star of the Baptist dancing rumor controversy. "It was very much a cultural thing. At that time Baptist, especially Baptist preacher boys did not dance. It happened like this. It was the junior/senior prom, and we had a gathering where everybody dressed up and went. Afterward they had a dance. They printed everybody's name in the paper who attended, and I do not know who started it, but somebody in our community picked it up and started running with it, saying that Gary West is a *dancing preacher*. It got to be a little bit embarrassing, so Glenn said, 'We will deal with this! Let me stand up in front of the congregation and tell them it's not quite what you read in the paper.' I remember it put some stress on my parents. I looked out on the congregation and my mother was crying, so I spoke to it and that seemed to end it, and there were no more repercussions or statements flying around."

Gary remembers, "Glenn got hot before and during the sermon. 'Y'all better stop this stuff, this gossip and slander!' He later debriefed sheepishly at the Wednesday night potluck. 'I think the rumor mill is working well in Wellington! Went to get mail at the post office. I met so and so who goes to the Methodist church, and they said 'Brother Glenn, I heard y'all had a real good service yesterday, and that things got kinda warm for the Baptists.' Glenn concluded, 'I guess if the Methodists are getting the word, the word is going around."

"I have often said over the years that he was the pastor that I needed through my high school years, and I state that because of where I am now. I have moved, as some would say, considerably to the left, and I am not saying that's where Glenn was. He was a traditional Southern Baptist in some ways, but he certainly didn't let it make a fool out of him. He was a very intelligent man and would offer good things from the pulpit and in his pastoral care. It was about that time when I was beginning to think that to preach was what I would like to do. He was just an excellent model for me, and so was Dorothy. I appreciated her, and I can still see her smile, and I never told her this, or never told anybody, but I could almost see a sense of mischief in her eyes. She was just a wonderful, full-of-life woman and could tease you or give you a hard time. I loved them both very much." (Gary West, Interview, 2016).

"The sermons, I cannot remember exactly what he said, but remember being used for a great deal of my life to rather loud, bombastic sermons. Various preachers who seemed to have only one or two or three lines to work from, but Glenn was not like that. He was always well prepared, and his content was different. It was a challenging kind of thought. It was something you could take away and chew on it a while. I remember one of our favorite people Mrs. Louis Ratliff, our high school English teacher, a member there at the church. I remember her saying one time that she had never heard a preacher pastor with the content that Glenn delivered. Every Sunday was something to work with if one would do that, and this was the time when I was beginning to think this was what I wanted to do. To watch him, his preparation and delivery was something very meaningful to me. He was completing his doctorate at that time, and I was not at the point then that I understood a person could go on to graduate studies, so I set my goal to one day get my graduate degree. He inspired me to pursue my doctorate at TCU, which I did in the late '70s and early '80s. Glenn put me on that track. (Gary West, Interview, 2016).

"Glenn was ecumenical in spirit and was always a bit brave. He also introduced me and the congregation to Dr. James Dunn and C.A. Roberts. He always brought in good people. There was another thing. I saw a healthy family. They genuinely loved each other, would tease each other in public. It was always an enjoyable time. Danny was all over the place. We (the youth group) always stayed too late on Sunday nights because it was fun times with Dorothy and Glenn. The congregation knew they wanted to serve and be missionaries. We knew that in time, we will lose them, but we can sure enjoy them while they're here. They also became friends with my parents, Oris and Laverne West, who were very grateful, and spoke of them until the end of their days." (Gary West, Interview, 2016)

On January 17, 1963, Dad received his Doctor of Theology in midwinter commencement at Southwestern Baptist Theological Seminary in Fort Worth, Texas. He and my mom announced to First Baptist Wellington that they had been approved as missionaries to Brazil and would be appointed May 14 in a service in Richmond, Virginia. After goodbyes with the Hickeys, Lybrands (who by now included my cousins Brenda and Michael Lybrand), and Thomersons in Arkansas, we set sail on August 19 from the Port of New Orleans on the *Del Sud* for Rio de Janeiro, Brazil.

Journey to Brazil on the Del Sud

Dad got plenty of colorful sermon material from our time on the *Del Sud*. "You never really understand this gospel story in Mark 6:46-50 (Jesus walks on the water during a storm that frightened the disciples) unless you have lived through a storm, especially a storm at sea.[13] When we traveled to Brazil in August of 1964, we traveled by ship. The *Del Sud* was a combination passenger and cargo ship in the Delta lines vessels sailing from New Orleans to various South American ports along the Atlantic Coast.

There were seventeen newly appointed missionaries aboard the Del Sud. On the third day of our seventeen-day journey we were advised that we would pass along the edge of Hurricane Cleo, which turned out to be a major hurricane of that busy season. Hurricane Cleo took the lives of 178 people, mostly Haitians and Cubans, and left behind nearly $200 million in property damage. Captain Smith put out a bulletin advising us that we would be passing through some pretty stormy seas for several hours but assured us that we would skirt around the edge of the storm and that there would be no danger except the possibility of some seasick passengers."

"Everybody has advice to give when it comes to riding out a storm at sea. Some people said, stay in your cabin, go to bed, and take plenty of dramamine. Others said, stay out of bed and walk around. Then there was one piece of advice from what was supposed to have been a real veteran of the seas. He said, 'Get out on the deck of the ship and get as close as you can to the prow of the ship. Face the waves and hold on for dear life. Just seeing the waves roll in will cure you of any seasickness.'

"Well, missionary Orman Gwynn (Orman and Elizabeth Gwynn, I.M.B. Missionaries, Brazil and Caribbean, 1964-2002) and I were foolhardy enough to take the advice. I think that was the poorest piece of advice I have ever heard in all my life! We made it through the storm, but on 'the edge of hurricane Cleo' was one shipload of seasick people."

Marlene and Ronnie Boswell gelled with the Hickeys and led the newbie missioners in their onboard entertainment. "The leadership at our home church had made a *wacheesy* board for us, and so we (Hickeys, Gwynns, Fleets, and Boswells) would go up on the deck at night and play. It was a cutthroat game. You could land on somebody and send them back to start over. This was right outside the bar, and soon other missionaries joined us and we were having so much fun that the people inside the bar came out and wanted to play!" (Marlene and Ronnie Boswell, I.M.B. Missionaries, South Brazil, 1964-1980)

"Crossing the equator on a cruise liner was a rite of passage Bacchus party. This is when the *polliwogs*, or first timers, passed thru the rituals of initiation (humiliation). In this case, we were required to kiss the hand and bow down to the Argentinian ambassador." Ronnie Boswell, Richard Walker (Richard and Beatrice Walker, I.M.B. Missionaries, Equatorial Brazil,1964-1972), and colleagues would not have this level of indignity, so conspired to throw the ship captain into the swimming pool in an audacious act of resistance. It didn't go over very well, except in the memories of the missionaries, who will always cherish being *polliwogs*. (Ruby Fleet, Interview, 2017; Ruby and Ray Fleet, I.M.B. Missionaries, North Brazil, 1964-1994)

The first trial awaited the new missioners shortly after they walked off the *Del Sud* into the *Cidade Maravilhosa* of Rio de Janeiro. A sumptuous meal was served by the veteran missionaries accompanied by sparkling champagne. All eyes of the vets were watching, intent on who would "when in Rome" drink it up. Timidly, being so far from their Southern Baptist roots, these tee-totaling deviants tasted what was a harmless *Guaraná* Antarctica berry drink. Raucous veteran laughter mixed with the innocent laughter of relief as the "You're not in Kansas Anymore" hardcore cultural adaptation began. (Ruby Fleet, Interview, 2017)

Baptists sent to a Catholic Hegemon

By 1963, when Mom and Dad were appointed, the I.M.B. was already expanding its orientation for new missionaries to include a month of cultural literacy, mission training and psychological tests, followed by a full year of intense Portuguese language school. No amount of orientation could prepare them for co-habitation with the largest Catholic culture on the planet.

The Jesuit missioners had been evangelizing successfully since 1549. Catholicism was omnipresent from baptism to burial, from Carnaval (Mardi Gras) to local and national patron Saint holidays. It held deep sway in all layers of culture with schools, hospitals and the unstated power of bishops and priests. Some priests were naturally territorial when the first Baptist missionaries showed up. This dynamic only began to change late in the 20th century with the rise of Brazilian Spiritism, Evangelical Protestants, and Pentecostals. Also contributing to the demographic shift was the courageous resistance that many Catholic priests and various Catholic based movements waged against the Military Dictatorship of 1964-1985. The status of Catholicism as the de facto State Religion began to erode.

Not until October 15th, 1882, did Southern Baptist missionary pioneers William Buck Bagby, Anne Luther Bagby, Zacharias Clay Taylor and Katherine Steves Crawford Taylor organize the first Baptist congregation in Brazil in Salvador, in the state of Bahia. Through providence or serendipity, their partner was an ex-Catholic priest named Antonio Teixeira de Albuquerque. Teixeira's journey from Priest to become the first Brazilian Baptist Minister and a consequential partner to the Missionaries is compelling to both Baptists and Catholics.[14]

David and Laura Spiegel are second generation missionaries who were granted tri-focal vision by their life story. They can see the missionary kid (MK), Missionary and Brazilian national points of view. David observes, "My recollection of my parents' ministry in Teresina (State of Piaui) is that most folks considered themselves Catholic; but practiced only at birth, weddings and funerals. I can remember that many were 'thirsty' for attention from whatever religion. So, as Brazilian members were trained to evangelize, those being evangelized were easily shown the 'way of the cross.'" (David and Laura Spiegel, MKs and I.M.B. Missionaries, South Brazil, 1979 to the present. David's parents Don and Betty Spiegel were I.M.B. Missionaries, North Brazil, 1959-90; Laura's parents Edward "Ed" Grady Berry and Lois Josephine Berry were I.M.B. missionaries, South Brazil, 1948 to 1985. Ed Berry was also a MK, son of Brazil missionaries William Hafford and Olga Anne Berry)

Years later, when Dad assumed the pastorate of Igreja Batista Central de Ibura (IBCI) in Recife, he was careful to build relationships with the Catholic Priest and the Assemblies of God Pastor of neighboring churches. Both were in sound decibel proximity to his sanctuary. The only relationship challenge was a productive negotiation with the Assemblies of God leadership to place their loudspeakers inside their church at key times.

There was not a warm relationship between the Campinas language school director and Dad's preaching gang of buddies. The director was a hardcore Presbyterian linguist who had strictly prohibited any translating of sermon texts from English to Portuguese as didactic damaging shortcut. He ranked the students with stars by their names for language proficiency achievement. Ronnie Boswell was not close to the top of this list. To right this wrong, he went to the local market and purchased enough stars to fill the achievement board to elevate everyone equally into the exalted heights of Portuguese proficiency. The director was livid with Ronnie and unhappy for most of the semester with Glenn Hickey, Orman Gwynn, and Richard Walker. They were told not to concern themselves with ministry and to focus on language learning.

A short time later, they were all offered opportunities to preach sermons by Dr. Thurmond Bryant, the professor of theology at the *São Paulo* Baptist Seminary and in charge of orientation for new missionaries. These proclaimers were nowhere close to mastery of Portuguese and had only two illegally translated sermons each. Sent out into the field with a love for proclaiming the gospel as their only communication tool, they delivered their agonized prose to perplexed listeners in the local congregations.

Once the lights went out on Dad. After a long prayer to stall, he lost his place in the sermon, so just started reading the text again from the beginning. After preaching outdoors at night by a kerosene lantern, Richard Walker showed up at the language school with no eye lashes because they had been burned off trying to read his sermon the night before. (Ronnie and Marlene Boswell, Interview, 2016)

A high point of the evangelical service that these missionaries provided to their Brazilian audiences was the invitation after the sermon, the opportunity to personally respond to the invitation for union with the transcendent God through Jesus Christ. This is the nexus of the service, like the Priest elevating the host to heaven before sharing it. Once it was Dad's turn to offer this gift to all. In his best flawed Portuguese, he said: "*Se quizer aceitar Jesus, levante um Mamão!*" It was Sunday market day, and there were many papayas present, so a guy in back proudly held up his papayas for all to witness. The crowd was amused. The difference is subtle:

Se quizer aceitar Jesus, levante uma Mão! If you want to accept Jesus, lift up your hand!

Se quizer aceitar Jesus, levante um Mamão! If you want to accept Jesus, lift up your papaya!"
(Orman Gwynn, Interview, 2016)

"Dr. Bryant frequently had to travel, so he asked Glenn and Ronnie to be co-pastors during his long absences. The longsuffering church members joked that they had three pastors: One absentee and the other two who could not speak Portuguese!" (Ronnie and Marlene Boswell, Interview, 2016)

Confronting Christ Who is Always There

After four years on the mission field in Northeast Brazil, Dad shared his disenchantment in a homily to seminary students and faculty at Southern Baptist Theological Seminary in Louisville, Kentucky.

"Those of us who go out to serve on the mission field find that there, too, we must confront the Christ who is always there. There are still a few people naive enough to think that the missionary, having surrendered himself to 'the highest calling,' has settled all accounts with the living Christ and therefore is rewarded with a life of perpetual bliss. Surely this view would have little chance of survival on an enlightened campus like this. Suddenly one is dropped into a choking wilderness of human need and misery. There is poverty, hunger, ignorance, filth, illiteracy, disease, and suffering on a scale unimaginable. None of which can be ignored by the sensitive disciple of Jesus Christ who knows that the gospel relates to all of life.

Do you see what to me is the most troubling, disturbing thing about Christmas? It is that the one who came at Bethlehem keeps coming back as He came to doubting Thomas, as He came to Peter on the shores of Gennesaret. He comes to disturb and to challenge. He comes to probe my innermost being as He did that morning with Peter: 'Do you love me Peter? Do you love me? Then feed my sheep.'"[15]

Declassified Information

Our experience as missionary kids (MKs) was often radically different from our missionary parents described by my dad above. MKs often have to recover from a host of pathologies that absent parents, overzealous families, boarding schools, and downright abusive adults inflict on their psyches. Our circle of MKs in Recife were lucky and blessed to have parents who not only had our highest good in mind, they allowed astonishing freedom to adolescents in a large and unpredictable city. As we matured and showed that we could handle our responsibilities, some of us were free to go on cycling, surfing, diving, and camping expeditions ahead of our time. We would take off on city buses, then on long treks hiking through sugar cane and coconut groves to find just the right paradise. A missionary *uncle* or *aunt* usually showed up to take us home about the time we were getting famished.

The missionaries became our family in Brazil, so we MKs called the missionaries uncle and aunt, not to be confused with my real Aunt Glenna, my father's sister, or Uncle Roy, my mother's brother. Only years later did we hear that not all the missionaries were so happy with this free-range parenting permission, but *O meu Deus!* (Oh my God!) what a magical journey from adolescence to adulthood we were granted!

Two sets of these wise parents were Uncle Dave and Aunt Glenda Miller (Glenda and Dr. David Miller, I.M.B. Missionaries, North Brazil, 1961-1992) and Uncle Fred and Aunt Bettye Spann. (Bettye and Dr. Fred Spann, I.M.B. Missionaries, North Brazil, 1962-1993) Glenda Miller was a native Californian, while Dave hailed from Philadelphia, PA. Neither Aunt Glenda nor Uncle Dave were from the traditional Southern Baptist Bible belt culture, which in the opin-

The Miller Family, circa 1974. Back row: Margie, Nancy, and Paul; front row: Aunt Glenda and Uncle Dave. Photo courtesy of Glenda Miller.

ion of Dorothy Hickey was quite refreshing. Dr. Dave Miller was Professor of Church Growth and Evangelism, and served as professor with Mom and Dad at the North Brazil Baptist Theological Seminary. *(Seminario Teologico Batista do Norte do Brasil—S.T.B.N.B)* and later as President of the Seminary. A Registered Nurse, Glenda served the poorest of the poor at the *Casa da Amizade*, the Baptist Friendship House. She also performed such unglamorous tasks as patiently administering forty rabies shots apiece to a few of us MKs who were bitten by runaway house-pet marmoset monkeys.

Cute and Capricious Marmosets. (Photo by Daniel Hickey)

Dr. Fred Spann was a pioneering music missionary and served as professor with Mom and Dad at the North Brazil Baptist Theological Seminary. His thirty-year ministry provided the model for mixing sacred music with Brazilian popular rhythms, taking choirs around the world. His brilliant blend of sacred and folkloric choral music enabled astonishing conversations with luminaries like Luis Gonzaga, the Brazilian popular musical icon of the 20th century. Uncle Fred and Aunt Bettye Spann opened their home to MKs whose parents served too far from the quality of education provided at the American School of Recife.

The Spann Family, circa 1970. Back row: James and Clay; front row: Suzanne, Uncle Fred, Grady, and Aunt Bettye. Photo courtesy of Wade Smith.

The Spanns usually had at least two boarders along with their own Jim, Clay, Grady, and Suzanne. Aunt Glenda and Uncle Dave, and their MKs Nancy, Margie, and Paul Miller often joined the Spann clan for excursions. This became a village, and whenever possible they took their broods plus guests out on kayaking, snorkeling, and surfing excursions into those alluring azure waters and coral reefs. The Hickeys were lucky on occasion to tag along.

This incomparable amount of fun had by MKs in Recife was strictly classified when our parents were on furlough and began asking for money to support their work through the *Lottie Moon Christmas Offering** for the International Mission Board. I was not allowed to include slides of our first-class frivolity on the beaches of northeast Brazil in my parents' missionary presentations. This now is all blissfully declassified information.

*In the 1800s, a missionary named Lottie Moon wrote letters from China urging American churches to fund more overseas workers. After Lottie's death on the mission field, the Women's Missionary Union began as an annual Christmas offering honoring her name, and to support international mission efforts for Southern Baptists. (From I.M.B. website)

Warm up and Taquaritinga do Norte Journey

A parent actually did accompany one of the first* of these epic adventures, the journey to *Taquaritinga do Norte* from *Recife* on bikes. That would be Dad. With a distance of one hundred and fifteen miles and a two thousand meters rise in elevation in tropical heat, it was a formidable journey even for dreamers like us. The collective imagination of Dad, and MKs Roger Turner (MK, parents Donald and Donna Turner, I.M.B. Missionaries, North Brazil, 1965–1983), Jim and Clay Spann, and myself took over.

We prepared by taking a warm-up trip to *São Lourenço da Mata* to see if we were ready for the big time. It was above ninety degrees and sunny, so Dad outfitted his Lawrence of Arabia neck protection. With the sunglasses, custom shorts, and racing top, it all worked for him, and with his Brazilian tan he looked like a styling Arabian sultan flying down the hills. On the outbound, a slow ascent though *São Lourenço*, his headgear caught the attention of the local children out flying their kites. One of them hollered, *"Olha o Sheik!"* (Look at the sheik!) That was all it took for him to develop a following, with twenty plus young boys yelling, *"Olha o Sheik!"* on his way up through the village. It was an uneventful ride until we returned through town, when the gravity shifted steeply in Dad's favor, and he sped down in front of the group. Now there were over fifty children chanting *Olha o Sheik, Pega o Sheik!*

Glenn and Dan ready for Taquaritinga do Norte, 1975

(Look at the sheik, catch the sheik!) Dad greeted and smiled with a thumbs up, then focused, head down, increasing speed with an up-side-down little boy grin looking back as the crowd closed in, and the rest of us were forced to stop and be friendly.

The epic day came and Dorothy Hickey, very keen to how these trips could go wrong, drove us to the Spann home and left us with hugs and a stern warning. "I am not going out to pick y'all up, so save some energy to peddle back. I already had to get up at four AM today, not planning on repeating that tomorrow."

Warning noted. In high hopes, we took off into the semiarid Brazilian northeastern landscape, excited as any youth could be with our relatively experienced adult guide, the Sheik. He wore his Lawrence of Arabia headgear and his unbounded optimism.

"Olha o sheik!, Pega o Sheik! Look it's the Sheik, catch the Sheik!"

We were psyched. The city quickly faded away, and the sparsely used highway of the day stretched out into infinity and beyond our dreaming legs. Oh, how little did we know what beyond infinity meant. By ten in the morning, we had already consumed a liter of water each, and the quick-fire muscle cell structure in our lower bodies was fading. It was hotter than even the Sheik anticipated, and before noon we were losing our optimism to arrive in *Taquaritinga do Norte* by sunset.

Lunch in the shade enabled our demeanor to temporarily abate into appreciation of the distance covered. Reality was not to hit until we re-mounted our bikes and felt the seats to be made of torture hardware. The long ride of youth's disillusionment began, and in less than an hour into the afternoon we wondered when it would ever end.

No one whined, but by three PM some were walking their bikes, secretly hoping for a lift. With about sixty miles to go, a couple of us compromised our values and grabbed the side hooks on slow moving trucks who offered to assist us in making the long climbs into the range. The tropical rainforests had long ago given way to the *Caatinga* vegetation and the semi-arid climate that claims so much life during the legendary droughts of Northeast Brazil. We asked for water at every stop and were drinking liters. Curious villagers observed with pathos, then laughter, as never had such thirsty and desperate *gringos* made a pilgrimage though these parts.

Nightfall, and our little band was stretched out for miles and now facing the serious two thousand meter climb up into *Taquaritinga do Norte*. No one was giving up either, if only to salvage some dignity and talking points. We reminded ourselves there was a swimming pool at our destination hotel.

The night turned to morning. With only moonlight to see the precipitous gravel road, we all made it. Yes, we all made it. We were too tired to swim and could barely crawl to our rooms.

Then Dad had to make one of the more difficult decisions of his life. Summoning all his courage, he called Dorothy Hickey for emergency back up the next morning. We all had a stony silent journey home, but thanks to my parents, one of the greatest adventures of our youth. This edgy bicycle trip became a powerful memory for Glenn and the young cyclists, retold as needed to reconfirm our courage to launch into the unknown with no certainty of the result. Venturing out on faith that risk falling off a tightrope with reason in pursuit of our better angels of daring, we discovered that it is this risk of faith that brings joy to the struggle.

*This story is one of a myriad tales of our MK life in Brazil experienced and knit into our beings like the smell of sea in our hair on the beach at night under the southern cross.

Dorothy the Mom

Adult reflection enabled me to appreciate what a fierce and devoted mother I had. She staged at least 2 interventions on my behalf that were spectacular in their results. When we were on furlough in Louisville, Kentucky, she was summoned into a meeting with gravitas called by the Principal of my school. Later she didn't admonish, but heaped instead on her son mighty unexpected praise. She discovered that I had finally punched a bully in the nose who had been calling me a "Brazil Nut" disparagingly all year in my 5th grade class. This was empowering.

She later sent up fervent prayers for my stature to increase when I was the shortest boy in my 8th grade class. Even as she later gave genetics its due respect, she believed those prayers were answered. With the size of the lunches she made for me to take to school, I could always trade up. Indeed, she was the sweetest mom I could ever hope for!

Mission Life in Recife, Brazil

"For me the hardest thing about being a missionary was having other people determine where we lived, what car we drove, or whether or not we could paint our house. One missionary colleague got very upset when the mission had promised a new larger car and gave them a smaller older model when they returned to Brazil from furlough. I agreed with their sentiments." (Glenda Miller, Interview, 2016)

Uncle Ray and Aunt Ruby Fleet and their MKs Vivian, Ray Jr. and later Patricia were our neighbors in a secluded palm-lined street in the *Casa Forte* neighborhood of Recife named *Jardin Carioca*. Uncle Ray was a Music and Religious Education Professor with Mom and Dad at the Seminary, while Aunt Ruby taught English and served as the Interim Business Manager for the mission for seven years. Mom said to me once "Your Aunt Ruby is so much smarter than anyone knows."

"The Mission had a famous square foot rule for housing, meaning there was a formula where the square ft. of the home had to match the family size." (Ruby Fleet, Interview, 2017) Our family was only three and Mom felt like we won the mission home lottery when they moved to *Jardin Carioca*. When asked about missionary living conditions in Brazil, she was eager to share her blessing with the people of her home church in Third Baptist Malvern, "She told me her house in Brazil was very nice." (Arkie Neal Remley, Interview, 2019)

As MKs, we were raised by a village of missionaries. After killing a young *sabiá-laranjeira* (Rufous-bellied thrush, a protected Brazilian songbird) with my brand new American-made BB gun, to which Aunt Ruby was a surprise witness, I confessed immediately. She took care not to judge but asked all the right questions to enable a reflection on my crime in such a way that I never wanted to hunt any living creature again.

Aunt Joan Varner, (Joan and Victor Varner, I.M.B. Missionaries, 1965-1971, North Brazil) Music Missionary and Professor at the North Brazil Baptist Theological Seminary, observed the expectations of hospitality: "I was teaching full time in the mornings and the afternoons and then trying to prepare meals. We almost always had company because we had one of the few houses that had an extra bedroom, so it was almost always full. I counted of the fifty-two weeks of one year, we had guests for fifty weeks. Recife was where anybody who had a problem with their car, anybody who needed to see the dentist, or anybody who needed to go to the mission office or the seminary stayed with one of the missionary couples. Nobody ever stayed in a hotel. It was just part of the expectation." (Interview, Joan Varner, 2019)

The International Mission Board

The International Mission Board, or I.M.B., in Richmond, Virginia (the Foreign Mission Board during the Hickeys' service) divided Brazil into three large missions covering a country larger than the continental U.S. Since a disproportionate amount of the Brazilian

Dr. Thomas Halsell, guest speaker at the annual North Brazil Mission Meeting, admires the five-year service pins presented to Dorothy and Glenn Hickey. Photo by Roberta Hampton.

population lived on the urban Atlantic seaboard, a majority of the I.M.B. missionaries to Brazil became urbanites. As mentioned earlier, the Board had a rigorous selection process that included an assessment of the mental health of the missionary candidates and a comprehensive cultural training adapted for each country. The first ordeal for Brazil mission candidates was the full year of intense Portuguese language study expected before any ministry assignment.

The Hickeys were part of the expansion of *Missionarios Norte Americanos* in Brazil. "That time frame 1964–1979 was the high point of missionary presence in Brazil. I remember that the joint Mission

Meeting in *Serra Negra* in 1982 of the three missions was overwhelming. Uncle Dan Burt, (Daniel and Mary Ellen Burt, Missionaries, South Brazil, 1957–1989) who oversaw securing the hotels, said that we had five-hundred and fifty missionaries/journeymen* present. With MKs, fifteen hundred would probably be a closer number." (David Spiegel, email, 2019)

When you sign up for a mission larger than your life, it sets up an unreliable and unpredictable metric for achievement. Mom, Dad, and their colleagues had the joyful and frustrating work of getting to define and redefine their expectations. They were accountable to the I.M.B. but at their best they tuned into the divine channel for affirmation, which often came in Portuguese.

*Journeymen (and Journeywomen) were two-year appointments of recent college grads that often cared for MK's, not jobs for the faint of heart.

Missionary Angst

"I am often asked the question, what's it like being a missionary? I always find that question difficult to answer because the answer I am prepared to give is often not the answer expected or wanted by the inquirer. Many people have romanticized or glorified the role of the missionary. Such a person expects the missionary to answer the question in glowing terms. He feels that the missionary has attained through his vocation and calling a life of perfect peace and contentment in the center of the will of God as though the will of God could be calculated mathematically.

"You know that many of our missionaries face real sacrifices in leaving family and friends behind to serve the Lord on some foreign field. We did not feel that we sacrificed anything to leave our country for Brazil. I am sure our parents felt that it was a sacrifice on their part. I only remember one time that I might have felt any distress for leaving home and friends. Not long after we had settled in Campinas,

Brazil for a year of language study, I awakened early one morning about 4 A.M. I suddenly sat up straight in bed, looked all around in the darkness, and said to myself, 'What in the world are you doing here in this place so far from home?'"[16]

FUTEBOL!

The MKs were swept into a love affair with *Futebol* (soccer), and they carried most missionary parents along with them. In 1970 every recently introduced color TV seared the most glorious moment into the country's collective heart. Brazil and its national treasure, *Pelé*, had defeated Italy 4–1 in Mexico City to become the only 3-time world champion, exalting the *Jogo Bonito* into the global imagination of at least a billion fans.

Dad and other preaching missionaries occasionally faced stiff competition for the people's attention during Sunday evening services in Brazil. Passion for favored soccer teams was chosen over listening to the sermon. Hidden radios and earphones made it possible to be present for the Sunday evening sermons in body only. Dr. David Mein, *S.T.B.N.B.* President during my parents' time in Brazil, and Pastor at *Igreja Batista do Cordeiro* (Baptist Church of the Lamb), carried immense authority just in his look. Occasionally, he paused his brief Sunday evening sermons to firmly rebuke a distracted fan in the pews. It usually only took one look. (David and Lou Demie Mein, I.M.B. Missionaries, North Brazil, 1944–1984)

DAY BY DAY

The beating heart of inspiration for the missioners daily service in a foreign land were the Brazilian nationals themselves. They were exuberantly grateful and expressed this warmly. At the core, they suspected that the *Americanos* had their best interest at heart, even as they bumbled along in bad Portuguese and launched uncertain projects for the sake of the gospel.

Glenn, Dorothy, and their colleagues carried on a host of activities and initiatives, and their days were as full as they could make them.

Dad was an introvert having to play the role of an extrovert, manifesting an equilibrium of humor and serenity that could only be broken by my mom's direct manner or the Recife traffic. Included in his days were early morning jogs, classes, meetings, ham radio intercontinental communication, hospital and church member visits, sermon preparation and study time, and chats with students and missionary colleagues. Mom's days were equally arduous, with a mix of teaching voice, rehearsing with choirs and mastering the art of shopping in open air markets and cooking from scratch. (By 1966 the convenience grocery store chain *Bompreço* arrived in Recife.) All this while both were driving *Rosa e Silva* and *17 de Agosto*, the primary arteries between the seminary and their residence. This task alone required intense focus since they shared these arteries with slow horse-drawn carts, slower human-powered carts, bikes, motorcycles, thousands of VW Bugs, and larger-than-should-be-allowed electric public trolleys that frequently became unhinged from their wires and blocked traffic for hours. Sundays were not for the day of rest. With two church services, Sunday School, and visitation in communities the missionaries were in high gear.

Usually all in for these challenges, Mom, Dad, and their colleagues were able to complete a surprising number of tasks throughout the day and accomplish their mission to inspire the Brazilian Baptist people and their churches to a generation of phenomenal growth in Brazil. They were innovative and pragmatic and able to accomplish their vision, often creating new projects and ministries that suited their talents, personality and audacity.

Bruce Oliver, (Bruce and Margaret Oliver, I.M.B. Missionaries, South Brazil, North Brazil, 1935–present) , Dale Carter (Dale and Sue Carter, I.M.B Missionaries, North Brazil, 1957–1993) and Orman Gwynn enjoyed the high life of missionary pilots as audacity *was* the job description. Dale and Sue Carter, Bruce and Margaret Oliver, and their families were stationed in *Corrente*, in the State of *Piaui*. Orman and Elizabeth Gwynn had a three-year assignment there in a long and illustrious career with the I.M.B. This was the legendary wild west cowboy and cowgirl mission destination, cherished by these hardy pioneers who found increasing abundant life and co-created with their Brazilian partners a thriving institute and Christian community. Dad was on the Board of Directors for the *Corrente* Baptist Institute, and relished his rarified flights in the CESSNA 206. PT-CFO and the CESSNA 337. PT-BUK to *Corrente* with these pilots. He treasured the stories of having to search for landing strips, emergency medivacs, or was just proud to be the one passenger who did not have to throw up inside his shirt because this was prayer inspiring turbulence.[17]

Fruit Highs

There are close to twenty-five varieties of fruits and berries native to Brazil and unknown to the North American palate until recently. Two of distinction are the *Pitanga* (Surinam cherry) and the *Caju* (the succulent yellow and red fruit on top of the raw cashew nuts.) A Sunday evening tradition after church upheld by our extended missionary family was to stop by *Que Delicia* Ice Cream shop for *Pitanga* sherbet, one of many delights. The taste bites and teases the tongue with a sweet citrus flavor to die for. Dad and I would stack two double cones, one at a time, so as not to allow a single precious drip on those humid nights. I suspected he may have even cut his sermons a few minutes short just to reach his heaven-on-earth a scoop sooner.

The tangy fibrous *caju* fruit is high in vitamin C and its juice has a delightful and sweet citric bite. Out from under the fruit grow cashews, or *anacardium occidentale*, in the same family as poison ivy and poison sumac. The raw casing holds the poison oils that have to be thoroughly roasted for hours to burn off. We had a cashew tree in the backyard and collected a bucket full of raw cashew nuts, of which we could not wait for local instruction to roast ourselves. The roasting took much longer than expected to get to the tasty export product. For hours into the night, Dad persisted over the vapors until he reached *castanha* nirvana. Chipping off the black charcoal revealed

The Pitanga (Surinam Cherry), the most delicious berry on planet earth, according to the author. Photo by Daniel Hickey.

The Caju fruit, with the dangerous cashew nut underneath. Photo by Daniel Hickey.

the ultimate prize inside, the warm tasty cashew nut. His reward the next morning were eyes swollen shut by the poisons and a rare day off from work to enjoy his toasty cashews.

First Brazilian Wedding

"I will never forget my first wedding I performed in Brazil. I think I have told you about the two words in Portuguese that were always so easy for me to confuse *diletos* (dearly beloved) and *delitos* (habitual felons). Instead of saying 'my dearly beloved' at the wedding ceremony I said, 'my dear habitual felons.' But that wasn't the worst part because I did not know a lot about the legal procedure in Brazil for religious weddings because in Brazil there is the religious wedding with the civil effect and then there is the civil wedding, and the legal documents are quite different. I didn't know that at the time, so that couple was 'living in sin' for at least a week until we got the papers worked out like they were supposed to be."[18]

PY7ZAA Come in, Over!

"Glenn liked to tinker with things and loved taking radios apart and putting them back together, just not always in the same way he found them." (Glenna Lybrand Interview, 2017)

Since his youth, Dad was captured by the power of daily curiosity in all things movable and transcendent. Electronics, scholarship, language, and physical fitness were always areas to be stretched, and each year offered new challenges. Cycling innovation in the form of new Italian *Campagnolo* Gear sets thrilled him. He was a life-long-learner in New Testament Greek, Portuguese, Spanish, German, and electronic nerdy innovations.

He was one of the first to be delirious in his community about the discovery and revelations of the Dead Sea Scrolls between 1949 and 1956. He gave PC classes to retirees in the 1990s, and he lived for the "aha" moments when truths and discoveries were revealed on a global scale. His excitement was poured into sermons and teaching illustrations, which he delivered with the passion and pleasure of these discoveries. At eighteen, he mastered Morse code and soldering minute electric boards for his ham radio, then stayed current with the state of new media in each decade, including reel to reel tape recordings, cassette tapes, VHS tapes, micro disks, video files, digital recordings, right up to Skype, which he was using the day of his passing in 2013.

Dad had already found his ham radio bliss back in college days. "Tommy Pernell was a close friend of Glenn and myself, and we strung a wire from one dorm to the other and began communicating in Morse code. We grew tired of learning our code during odd hours, but Glenn didn't. He went on to learn the code, how to send it, how to read it, and the technology (behind it). He got his license.[19]

No other instrument captivated him more than ham radio, and he was quick to put this passion into the service of missions. He never saw a ham radio antenna he did not appreciate and custom designed one for his missionary residence in Recife, Brazil.

It is difficult to relay the urgency and delight of 1960s and '70s international ham radio communications to the modern mind. Phone calls were exorbitant, and letters took months to arrive between Brazil and North America. Ham radio became the lifeline between families and could make the difference in getting life changing news across continents. "This is PY7ZAA" became a call sign introduction known in ham circles around the world as Dad eagerly embraced a "ministry of connection" between all manner of parties.

The Hickey home was full of visitors at odd hours, waiting for the word on a birth or the passing of loved ones. "Over" was the magic word, uttered into the atmosphere of anxious anticipation, followed by the interminable silent seconds of angst when a human response could change a life direction or immediate plans. "Yes, the Spann adoption was approved, over." "Your daughter was accepted into Baylor, over." "Your father was released from the hospital, over." Joy and sorrow often mixed as the life events were shared over the magical air. Aunt Ruby Fleet next door, a quick study, got her Morse code-

"This is PY7ZAA, over."

certified license and joined the international ham club. She, Orman Gwynn and a long list of missionaries maintained the worldwide network of free daily communications, often sharing the day's news and prayer requests in evening ham radio chats.

A favorite child of President John F. Kennedy's Alliance for Progress was the people-to-people component Partners of the Americas, where every country or state in Latin America was matched with an American state. Pernambuco state in northeast Brazil was matched with Georgia. The Georgia/Pernambuco partnership of the 1970s and 80s was a model program, engaging many of the best professionals in both states to make a direct positive difference in the lives of their hemispheric neighbors.

PY7ZAA became the point of entrée into the Recife leadership of the Georgia/Pernambuco Partners of the Americas. Dad's primary phone patch buddy in Atlanta was another "Woody," and the two coordinated the details of six citizen exchanges between Georgia and Pernambuco, cumulating with the visit by Georgia Governor Jimmy and First Lady Rosalynn Carter in 1969.

"The Georgia/Pernambuco Partnership was one of sixty partnerships in the Partners of the Americas Program that pairs forty-six regions and states with all thirty-one countries located in Central, South America, and the Caribbean. Designed to foster friendship and understanding between people from the two units in each partnership, the program involves people in intercultural exchanges and encourages them to work together on mutually agreed-upon programs to promote social, economic, and tech development." (Source Booklet, 25th anniversary, Georgia/Pernambuco Partners).

This was the new and magnificent cause for Dad to dedicate his best efforts, wide-eyed to the synergistic crossing of the civic and spiritual self, for which he was fully equipped to pair his sacred mission

The Pernambuco Partners as guests of Rosalynn Carter in the White House.

and the Georgia/Pernambuco Partners in that magical time. President Carter and First Lady Rosalynn did not forget the Recife Partners and invited them for a White house visit in 1977, their first year in office. Dad was asked to lead that delegation with Recife Partners President Carlos Fernandes, and had a peak experience as the only Southern Baptist American from Recife, Brazil visiting a Southern Baptist First Lady who loved the people of Recife!

It was during that time that Dad suggested I look into a career as a diplomat, which was freeing to a PK/MK who had no desire to be a preacher. When I was a freshman student at Ouachita Baptist University in 1975, he would wake me up from Recife with a phone patch from Woody in Atlanta on Sunday mornings, I suspect so I would not miss church.

Dorothy's Highlight: Singing for the Carters

"The state of Pernambuco entered into an exchange program with Georgia during the 1970s. In 1974 as part of the program, the governor asked us to organize a fourteen-voice choral group (*O Folcoral*) to present native popular music as well as some historical works from Pernambuco. One of the tour's highlights was presenting a forty-five-minute concert for the Governor and Mrs. Jimmy Carter. Brazilians excel in making themselves at home, so in the informal setting of the ballroom of the mansion, they sang beautifully." (Dr. Fred Spann memoirs)

Mom rarely talked of public figures except for Jimmy and Rosalynn Carter. She loved re-telling the story of the couple's humble simplicity in sitting down on the floor close and directly in front of the group, deeply moved by the Northeastern Brazilian rhythms.

Missionary Colleague Reflections on Glenn and Dorothy

"Glenn was a dear friend, and he responded in kind to me and took me on as a brother missionary. I remember him riding his bike to *Silvania* (the Baptist camp).He was a solid, kind man. He didn't go off on tangents. He was a friend of everybody who would let him be, and he had a lot of wisdom and down-to-earth common sense, which he applied in his mission work. Dr. David Mein laid the foundation and was the secret to the success of the North Brazil seminary. Glenn's teaching ministry thrived during that era because he understood Brazilians, and was one, basically," Byron Harbin. (Byron and Dora Ann, I.M.B. Missionaries, South and North Brazil 1975- to 1998)

Dr. Fred Spann could not believe the news of the Hickey's appointment. "One of the most interesting coincidences in our lives occurred as we learned that two college friends were being appointed to the *S.T.B.N.B.* in Recife, Glenn and Dorothy Hickey. They were a couple of years ahead of us at Ouachita, but we knew them albeit from afar. As a fan of one of the most popular singing ensembles on campus, the Ouachita Quartet, I admired the baritone Glenn and the quartet's close-knit harmony and terrific showmanship. Dorothy was soloist with the Ouachita Choir, which I joined during my first year at OBU.

"We felt so very fortunate to have two more 'Arkies' in Recife at the seminary. Glenn was an excellent professor of New Testament in theology. He had studied Portuguese seriously in order to speak and preach correctly. Dorothy became a wonderful colleague in the Music Department. Being a soprano, she taught some of our early female students vocal techniques. She was especially effective because her musical capabilities allowed her to accompany them on the piano during lessons.

"Glenn also was interested in applying the truths he taught to seminarians by becoming an active pastor in *Ibura* (government housing project community). Future ministers could emulate his example as they proclaimed God's word, they had learned with him and observed how to administer a local church. What I appreciated about

Glenn was that he never let his knowledge, scholarship, or theology keep him from shepherding a new church, which he did at *Ibura*.

For her part, Dorothy graciously consented to serve as pianist in the church where we raised our family, the *Igreja Batista do Cordeiro*. Our congregation thrilled as she filled in chords and emphasized accurate rhythms with her enthusiastic keyboard flair. She could invigorate any congregation to sing joyfully to the Lord. She also performed the soprano solos as our church choir presented Dubois'

"Our congregation thrilled as she filled in chords and emphasized accurate rhythms with her enthusiastic keyboard flair." Dr. Fred Spann. Full disclosure: This is a blend of two photos by artist Sarah Senseman Mack—Dorothy Hickey leading congregational music, and the MK choir practice at a North Brazil mission meeting, circa 1970, with Dr Fred Spann directing.

'Seven Last Words of Christ' on local TV, a pattern many evangelical churches later followed." (Dr. Fred Spann Memoirs)

My mom became known for her direct manner, which proved useful on the mission field. "There are people that you can talk to, and you never know where they stand on anything. That was not the case with Dorothy. She was hospitable, open, cordial, and so talented. The music gave her an upper hand with the language, too. She improvised in the kitchen very well, learning to use the local spices in her cooking." (Ruby Fleet, Interview, 2017)

Rocky Raccoon Finds Gideon's Bible

The yearly North Brazil Mission meetings were boring affairs for MKs. Our parents made budget and other momentous decisions, and we had just enough supervision to stay clear of trouble. *Itaparica*, an island resort in Bahia state, was a radical departure, and included a five-start beach and swimming pool. It was only in the interviews for this work that I discovered the person responsible for our upgrade was Aunt Bettye Spann, who was on the committee who gave us that paradise. Up until then the bright spot had been Uncle Fred Spann's MK choir practices, usually accompanied by my mom. We learned and performed the newest catchy tunes by composer Buryl Red.

The year was 1975, the last Mission Meeting for our group of MKs, and we were in festive spirits. The marquee event was the family talent show. Mom and Dad actually had drama in their past, performing Homer and Jethro skits for the youth of First Baptist Wellington, Texas. Before the trip, I had selected my favorite Beatles' tune from the *White* album, "Rocky Raccoon," just in case I was able to talk them into presenting it as a mini-musical melodrama for the show. To my amazement, they accepted. (They had grown weary of my habitual playing of "Why Don't We Do It in The Road?" at excessive volumes on the home turntable, so "Rocky Raccoon" was a nice respite.) We rehearsed once. Dad was Rocky, Mom was his girl Magill, and I was the villain who shoots Rocky after stealing his girl.

It worked! We received a huge ovation. I think having Dad wear a coonskin cap and falling back on his Gideon's Bible won over the non-Beatle missionary fans in the room. It was a flash moment when I realized my parents were both luminous and humble.

We thought we might have first place locked up until the stunning all blonde Shultz family did a number with Von Trapp family "Sound of Music" charisma. Darn them, we got second place! We were all together still basking in the glow of our stardom when Clay Spann stole the evening by streaking across the large banquet hall. He ran over and over to the amplified tune of Ray Stevens *The Streak* as he loosely held *The Streaker* sign over his *sunga* (immodest Brazilian men's swimwear). The shocked laughter built up to a falling-out-of-your-chair volume, and the applause was for an encore.

"Mission meeting was never the same after that." Stan Schochler, (MK, Parents Melba and Lowell Schochler, I.M.B. Missionaries, South and North Brazil,1962-1995)

The Brazilian Experience of the Professors

By 1967, Mom and Dad had come into their full pedagogical gifts at *S.T.B.N.B.* The Seminary President, Dr. David Mein, a Brazilian MK himself, was a statesmanlike authority in Portuguese and English. He inspired the confidence of both traditionalists and progressive thinkers in the docent core. Dad had grown a mustache, and with his bronzed look and fluid Portuguese could fool many a new student into thinking he was Brazilian. He grew into the good graces of so many students that he was named *Paraninfo* (professor of the year) by the graduating class of 1967.

Mom had conquered her early challenges in Portuguese and enjoyed her voice students immensely as they enjoyed her soprano. Her joy were voice students like Argentina Lopes and Lourdes Nogueira. "Professor Dorothy played a special role in my musical formation. She was an efficient teacher and great friend." (Argentina Lopes, studied voice with Dorothy Hickey, 1967-1969)

A Professora Dorothy Hickey, circa 1967

After her studies with Mom, Lourdes Nogueira eventually went on to earn her Doctorate in voice at North Texas State University. Her memories are effervescent: "My voice teacher Dorothy acted like she never expected to become a Missionary. She had a pure and generous heart and acted unaware of the immense talent in her possession. Never overtly religious, she just lived life to the fullest. Humble and spontaneous, she had fun with all of us. She would sit in the Seminary Chapel without a hymnal, and play the most amazing arrangements, we were overwhelmed! Professor Dorothy multiplied herself into many Dorothys. Whoever passed through her went on to plant in other places." (Dr. Maria de Lourdes Nogueira, studied voice with Dorothy Hickey 1967–1969.)

Cafézinho-Brazilian coffee break with S.T.B.N.B. professors: (facing) Chaplain and Professor Ademar Paegle, Professor José Almeida Guimarães, Professor Glenn Hickey and Professor Ray Fleet; (back to camera) Professor Camaliel Perruci and Professor Lívio Cavalcanti Lindoso. Photo courtesy of Missionary Wade Smith.

Former Student Marconi Monteiro Reflects

"Between 1974 and 1978, Dr. Hickey was my professor of Greek and New Testament Theology. He taught me how to study the Bible from both a critical and devotional perspectives. I learned how the Bible was formed, the historical context in which it was written. He enabled tools to develop a critical perspective on themes that many times people unnecessarily make controversial like questions of authorship, dates, the absolutism of certain doctrines. He helped me a great deal to see the Bible, especially the New Testament, in its totality. He introduced great students of the Bible to me, such as Gerard Vom Rae, a very capable German theologian, and the study of Greek, essential to understand the Biblical texts.

There is a temptation in the Christian world to mystify the Bible, as if it was perfect. You cannot find one discrepancy, not one shadow of error. There is a way of thinking out there—The 'inerrant interpretation of scripture,' and he helped us demystify the Bible, to accept it as the word of God, without having to place it *em Pe de Igualdade com Deus* (on par of equality with God).

"So, we see that God used men as the agents, people who themselves had historical limits, their own thoughts, even so the holy fingers guided them to bring the message of God to us. So certain texts have obvious historical limits, and we must interpret them to bring their message to our times. So I have profound respect for what Dr. Hickey taught me. He was a patient professor. I never saw him lose his calm center in any circumstance, and I know I was *muito chato* (a very irritating student). He was a person that worked biblical texts to their depths. He was open, always fair in his way of dealing with students, and my enjoyment of the academic aspect of biblical study started with him. I still enjoy in the fruits of intellectual freedom when I open a Biblical text.

"He was generally well received by all, and I cannot remember any controversies. At that time, Dr. David Mein encouraged an atmosphere of intellectual stimulation, debate, and academic freedom partnered with a seriousness for ministry.

"I have a profound respect for him and own a good part of my ability to think theologically to him. In fact, the missionaries from Dr. Hickey's generation had a great impact on the work of theology in Brazil. They dedicated themselves to the future theological and pastoral leadership of the country. His generation was not competitive with Brazilian leadership but insisted on being collaborative. They saw their role as supportive. It also is very beautiful to see the effect that Brazilians had on that generation of missionaries. I can see that when they talk about their memories of relationships with the people of the churches, both the missionaries and the MKs exude such joy in their memories of that time. Teaching is an art and a science, and Dr. Glenn was a master of mixing both."

"When I arrived at the North Brazil Baptist Theological Seminary, I met several people who struck me by their conduct. When I first met Professor Hickey, we became friends. He was an American/Brazilian. I noticed his facility for relationships. He had no prejudice. Even his way of being was Brazilian, and something that caught my immediate attention was his fluency in Portuguese. Even his physical appearance was Brazilian, and he turned into an exegete. He had a tremendous dominance of biblical Greek. He established a dialogue with his students and was open and attentive. He was a true university professor. He did not impose, but lectured in a dialectical way that captivated students. He was a deeply appreciated professor, avoided monologues and allowed the students to relate with him. He respected the personalities of each student. If you observed this style, you would see that eventually the students also opened up. He specialized in the parables, had a relationship with the German theologian *Joachim Jeremias* and was influenced by the idea of needing to contextualize these passages to our current days. It was a refreshing approach to ask 'What is this parable saying to me, to us, in our day and time?'

"I was the chaplain of the seminary and frequently invited him to be the guest preacher. It was the day that the chapel would usually fill up to hear him because he was a positive exegete of the New Testament Greek and could preach profoundly.

"The International Mission Board out of Richmond, Virginia, which commissioned Dorothy and Glenn in 1964, had a training guide that was written to enlighten missioners on the difficult task of entering new cultures with sensitivity. Hickey had read the manual on how to immerse oneself in the culture because he did it without reservation, even entering our games with zest. His Portuguese was native, and he understood the nuances of our way of life. He loved our foods, the *Bossa Nova* music, and was deeply in tune with the politics of the day. An unspoken badge of honor among the Brazil missionaries was reserved for those who could learn and master Portuguese as adults. Glenn was able to leapfrog into native fluency within a year and was interpreting for visiting *Norte Americanos* within two."

REFLECTIONS OF JAIRO ALVES DA SIQUEIRA,
FORMER STUDENT AND CURRENT PASTOR

"Dr. Glenn Hickey was a master teacher! I have often contemplated his spontaneous and friendly manner, so sincerely joyful in his way of being. As a professor he had good teaching practices,

Class preparation time at Seminario Teologico Batista do Norte do Brasil. Inspired by original photo, Roberta Hampton.

and a mastery of the content. He was respectful to everyone and creative and enjoyed what he was doing. His classes always were attractive even with the most complex content. His charism was to calmly explain each detail and know how to evaluate each student according to how they understood the materials. My time with him was brief, but it was sufficient to grasp the most that I could from his knowledge.

"According to Saint Thomas Aquinas, 'There are people who seek knowledge just to know more, and this is curiosity; others seek knowledge to gain fame, and this is vanity, others to grow, and this is prudence, and still others seek it in order to build up others, and this is love.' I believe this was the motive of Professor Glenn Hickey. So, my word is gratitude and admiration for what he was, fulfilling his vocation to teach the word of God and to be a great collaborator with the Baptist work. I learned from him."

Preaching from the Portuguese New Testament at IBCI, Bairro do Ibura, Recife.

There is an inspirational founder to the *Igreja Batista Central do Ibura* (Central Baptist Church of Ibura), or IBCI, as current members call it, and his name is Victor Varner. Missionaries Joan and Victor Varner, and their MK daughters Lynn and Jan arrived in Recife in May 1967.

The Hickeys and Varners hit it off since they had common roots in Arkansas/Oklahoma culture, or maybe it was a destiny of seren-dipity. Aunt Joan and Mom were both deep into piano and voice, while Victor, in addition to teaching church administration at the seminary, got busy starting a new church way out where the Recife bus line ended. These were government satellite housing projects called Ibura 1, 2, 3, 4 and 5, and a church planter's dream com-munity. Uncle Victor was an overachieving missionary and built the spiritual and concrete foundation for IBCI. In a metaphor of sacrifice, Victor Varner and the founding members created a thriving com-munity even as he sustained a back-injury lugging fifty-pound cement bags up narrow ladders to pour the roof.

The Varners returned stateside for treatment of his back, leaving with *saudades* (a blend of nostalgia and homesickness, fully ex-pounded on page 85) of their times in Brazil. As he was leaving Brazil, Uncle Victor had invited my dad to preach at *IBCI*. For Dad, this be-came fortuitous, then a joyful destiny! He later accepted the pastorate and thrived there for ten years. Victor Varner passed into the light in 2015, and his memory is cherished and memorialized by the grateful *IBCI* community.

"Courage starts with showing up and letting ourselves be seen."[20] Dr. Brené Brown, a research professor at the University of Houston, has made it her life's work to study the connections between courage and vulnerability. Glenn, Dorothy, and their colleagues were practic-ing this art of daring when diving into the humanity and struggle of Brazilians in the process of economic exclusion. They would call it "being the hands and feet of Jesus." Dad went from being Pastor Glenn to brother Glenn in homes, church life, and long hours of immersion into the community. He allowed himself to be seen by his church members, and perhaps this vulnerability was his greatest secret. These accounts are simple experiences of members who ate, drank, laughed, and even slept in the same room at church camp with *o nosso Pastor.*

"A little story about our pastor, Dr. Glenn Hickey. He was my pastor during childhood and adolescence. I remember him fondly because he was always very sensitive and highly valued the work of the young girls in *Mensageiras do Rei* (Girls in Action or G.A.s in the S.B.C. churches), the organization I was a part of. I will always cherish how he comforted me in the week before my Baptism when I broke my arm, and I was sad. I also remember when he returned to Brazil he expressed such joy to be with us again!" (Joana D'arc "Darquinha," IBCI Member)

"I was a member during the time of Pastor Glenn. Both my parents and all nine of my siblings except one brother were baptized by the pastor. Pastor Glenn was the first pastor for our family, and he was dedicated, helpful, loving, and gave focused attention to everyone. I remember that during my childhood, the pastor brought many donations of milk and other basic foods, since we were a very large family and struggled at times. We have always been so grateful for how he helped us. We so enjoyed accompanying him for house-to-house visits and evangelism. Even the children like tagging along. We covered many neighborhoods with our pastor. We missed him very much when he had to return to the United States. I was baptized on March 9, 1974, and was thrilled not only to be baptized but to receive a Bible from the dear pastor." (Ester Viana, IBCI Member)

"Our Sister Vilma admired Pastor Glenn for the elegant way he dressed and for his snazzy boots. We all remember at the church retreat where everybody had to sleep in double bunks on a rainy night. Our Sister Valeria loves to tell when the Pastor slept on the men's side on the lower bunk with my little brother on the top. The next morning Pastor Glenn said in curious voice, 'I do not understand, why I am all wet down here on the bottom bunk?' The group's uproarious laughter and the legend of the pastor who sleeps in the same room with everybody grew as did Glenn's realization that the culprit was not the rain." (Valeria, Vilma and Vera Fernandes, sisters, and founders, IBCI).

"I remember there were two blind siblings in the church, Edelsio and Eneide, who were also great accordion players. Pastor Glenn had a great amount of attention reserved for them, and when they didn't show up for church, he would send someone to go bring them." (Vera Fernandes, IBCI member)

Dad later told of being inspired by these siblings of the Costa-Reis family. "It was my privilege to be acquainted with a blind family in the church where I served for nine years. Three of the four members of the Costa-Reis family were blind. Only one enjoyed eyesight, and because he was the only breadwinner in the family, he was away from home most of the time driving a city bus. The hours that he was home were out of necessity mostly spent resting so he could get up and go to work again. Their home was for all practical purposes a home that functioned without eyes. I visited in that home quite frequently and would often go on Sunday evenings to pick up a young woman and young man in their late twenties and take them to Training Union (Evening Sunday School), church, and then back home.

"In these contacts, I learned a lot about the life of blind people who live, physically at least, in a world of total darkness. I was amazed at the way they moved about in their little three-room house, how they had those landmarks all around that their fingers could touch and identify immediately where they were in that home. I was in total fascination one evening as I sat and watched the young lady prepare a meal for that family and set it on the table. I shared that meal with them. I was amazed at how the young man learned to play the accordion so beautifully, an instrument he had never seen in all his life, and his eyes had never beheld a sheet of music.

"I was amused one evening when I went to pick them up in a new car that the mission had provided me, and to notice how quickly they observed its newness. They didn't see it with their eyes, but I was amazed at how quickly with the smell that car, the touch of it, and how their ears heard the purr of a new motor, and immediately they knew because they had learned to see in another way. I learned a lot about the tragedy of blindness by contact with that family, but I also was made to think about a greater tragedy, and that is the tragedy of many, many people who are unable to see what really matters in life."[21]

Elisabete Tavares, a founding member, was the rock who enabled the missionary tag team transition from Pastor Victor to Pastor Glenn. In 2019 she reflected on Dad's years as Pastor:

"Between 1969 and 1979 under the tenure of Pastor Glenn, eight youth were sent to study at the North Brazil Baptist Theological Seminary, six of whom are current pastors serving in other states in Brazil. We also formed a thirty-voice choir and organized women and girls mission teams.

"He initiated various evangelistic campaigns and new congregations, coupled with full support of social action ministries that blessed the community. Pastor Glenn, even while carrying a full load teaching at the seminary, was with us Sunday morning and evening, preaching and winning souls for Jesus. On Wednesday evenings, he taught Christian doctrine to the whole church. He visited the members in their homes frequently, even members who had moved far out of state. Sister Maria Duailibe, who got married and moved to Rio de Janeiro, and sister Maria Aureliana, who became a widow, and moved with her children to live in São Paulo both received visits from the Pastor, which made a joyful difference in their lives.

"I affirm that in all the years that he served at IBCI, Pastor Glenn contributed to the development of God's kingdom, recognizing that all glory, honor, and praise is to God." (Tribute by Elisabete Tavares, written for the 50th anniversary of IBCI on May 18th, 2019)

Dad also enabled the first Royal Ambassador chapter at IBCI for young men, which bears his name, "Embaixadores do Rei Dr. Glenn Hickey."

The people of IBCI stayed with Dad long after he left Brazil. "I know people at my church in Ibura in Brazil who were living somehow on a salary of fifty to one-hundred dollars a month. God made it possible for those people to give, to build a building, and then to build another building. Out of that deep poverty, the grace of God abounded, and those people were able to give. There was no give-to-get-rich scheme there, I will tell you for sure, but I saw some people's lives blessed and enriched in many other ways, as God operated in their lives and gave them spiritual wealth and riches and joy and satisfaction that they had never felt before. I believe that's the way God works in our lives."[22]

Parable of the Waiting Father According to the Father

As a PK and a MK, the cautionary tale of the prodigal son (Luke 15:11-32) was inescapable, and in my long experience of pew-sitting used as a warning to not detour too far from the Baptist road. Much later I heard it preached as an unmasking of the judgmental older brother, which I enjoyed heavens more! Our family lived a version this story and expanded the narrative into the heroic mother's point of view.

"For about nine hours in a very strange place on the other side of the world, I had a lost son. My son Danny and I were returning from the Baptist World Alliance in Stockholm, Sweden, and we were in the city of Rome, Italy on that particular day. We ate lunch at the coliseum on our way back to the train station and stopped by a park to look around. Danny went around another way to take some pictures, and before we knew it, we were lost from each other. He assumed that since we were going together to the train station that we would get together there, and I assumed that since we got separated in the park that we would eventually get back together in the park. So I waited about two hours, and when no one appeared, except a lot of kooky characters who made me wonder what went on in that place and what kind of entity was in control of that park. Well, after about two hours, I decided to go to the train station, and you know how those things work. Danny decided he would come back to the park. We didn't come the same way, of course, and he was at the park looking for me while I was in the train station looking for him.

"After coming back, I had no other choice but to notify the Rome police and the American embassy that my son had disappeared. I spent about four hours in the central police station of Rome and saw that parade of all kinds of unsavory characters coming in there and being booked. About 9 o'clock, the detective began looking at his watch and said to me that the station was going to close. I did not know what to do. Danny did not have his passport or any identification or telephone number. He didn't even have enough money to purchase bus fare. He had no idea where we were staying at a Baptist orphanage.

"I was desperate, and had contacted the missionaries, and about 9 o'clock a wonderful Italian Baptist pastor came to that police station. He and his good wife took me to their apartment nearby, and we settled in for what looked like might be an all-night vigil, waiting for some word from the police station. Finally, about 10:30 that night the call came from the Baptist orphanage where we were staying that Danny had arrived safe and sound.

"A lot of things can go through your mind in a situation like that, and if you have ever been there you know. It was nine hours of wondering and waiting with all kinds of questions running through my mind. Is he safe, is he alive, has he been kidnapped, is he lying in the bushes where someone knocked him out, has an automobile hit him, or is he in the hospital? Well, I learned a little bit that day about what it's like to have a lost son, and I think it gave me a better appreciation of the story of the prodigal son because you see it helped me see the other side of the story. We call it the parable of the prodigal son. Jesus did not call it that. Some have suggested that we call it the parable of the waiting father."[23]

Accordin to the "Lost" Son

In 1975, Dad decided it might well be his last chance to create a father/son memory trip before my college years, so after extensive negotiation with Mom and months of meticulous planning with maps scattered about the house, we were off to a 10-country EU-rail adventure. Off is a good word for it since we followed no tour groups and frequently took the wrong trains. Since the EU-rail was all free for a month, it didn't matter. We learned to plan round-trip overnights out and back to the same destination just to get a free place to sleep. We ate mostly cheese, fruit, and bread since this was recommended in [Fodor's Europe on Five Dollars a Day] guidebook.

By the time we hit Italy, we had either hiked, cycled, or Euro-trained through nine countries and thought ourselves savvy. We did stop by the Baptist World Alliance in Sweden which was good cover for Dad as a Southern Baptist missionary. While he attended long meetings, I experienced unsavvy attempts to visit with Swedish female people. They did not care to speak Portuguese or English.

Dad had purchased *La Scala* Opera tickets in Rome as a finale for the trip. It was set for the evening, and that day we had a casual lunch in the *Villa Borghese* park. He said was going to check out an electronic store he saw off the park, and since I had no interest, he asked me to stay put. I did so, and after waiting the prescribed polite 15 minutes, I headed over to an irresistible soccer jersey store I had seen earlier. When I did return to the park, of course Dad was not there, and with no plan B in the pre-cell phone era, our separation began.

I had no money. After several attempts at begging, (my gringo looks did not impress Italians as an authentic beggar's profile) I sat in the *Futebol* storefront and started a conversation in *Portu-Italiano* about global soccer fortunes with a hard-core fan. After my begging confidence returned, I ask him for a bus fare, this time authentically desperate. He gladly gave more than enough. *"Grazie! Grazie! Grazie!"* ("Thank you" repeated so many times that my benefactor raised his hands for me to stop.)

So amazed was I by this generosity, and by my hazy memory of the bus stop close to our Italian Baptist host family, that it felt like the best day of my life. Preparing myself to be at least embarrassed by my father, I was secretly proud of finding my way home. My shock was intense to witness not only a multifamily prayer vigil initiated by my dad, but the free flow of Baptist Italian wine mixed with sacred hymns, all in celebration of my being "found." (I was allowed a token taste and never grieved missing the opera.)

During this time Mom planned her own excursion with the Spann family to *Corrente, Piauí* to lead a music conference with Dr. Fred Spann. "Once Dorothy traveled with our family to *Corrente*, about one thousand miles distance. From Recife, we drove to *Petrolina* in one day (about five hundred ninety-three miles) and from there we drove about twenty-eight hours on dirt roads with potholes. The brakes failed on our Chevrolet Carryall, but we arrived safely but dusty (no, in reality, really filthy!) and totally exhausted. Dorothy taught several students basic piano techniques for a week and accompanied the choir made up of all those who attended. About three hundred people took various classes in music. It should be noted that several of them came later to the seminary to follow their calling to spread the Good News through music. (Dr. Fred Spann Memoirs)

Mom came home to Recife to face another test of courage. Dad discovered in a sobering transatlantic phone call that she had a larger adventure than we, and that she had been alone at home when weeks of tropical rains swelled the three rivers that met the equatorial Atlantic high-tides and produced the largest floods in Recife's history.

She was caught at our *Casa Forte* neighborhood home, which was two kilometers from the *Capibaribe* River. The most eerie event was watching a pack of large rats run up our cobblestone street and climb walls of *congongol* (ceramic lattice) outside our upstairs porch. She took refuge with Aunt Ruby Fleet next door, and they both had to stay on the second floor for almost twenty-four hours until the waters receded. It was Mom's lot to clean up the half-meter-thick muck and trash containing dead rats in our home by herself and then lock it all up. She faced alone the loss of heirloom furniture and a twenty-year accumulation of now-dead ham radio ham equipment. It was not a fun phone call for Dad, who in the midst of celebrating his son found, suddenly heard of the losses and challenges Mom faced. "If I were to use one word to describe Dorothy it is that she was exceptionally brave, doing it all alone without the men folk." (Ruby Fleet Interview, 2017)

The Lecio Wanderley Surprise
"How Big is your World?"

"Lecio Wanderley is one of those students you look at and wonder if he will ever amount to anything for the Lord. He never seemed to have a serious thought. He didn't take his studies seriously. I never expected much from Lecio. When I heard he was in the States studying at Southwestern Seminary, I thought he had just found a way to get a good job and live the easy life in the good old U.S.A. But one day, long after we left Brazil, I picked up my Southwestern Seminary Alumni magazine, and there was a big picture of Lecio, a seminary graduate, with a degree in Christian Recreation, with a bunch of street kids in Recife, Brazil. You have probably read about the serious problem of street kids in Brazil, kids abandoned or orphaned. They are left to wander the streets, begging and stealing, living off scraps from garbage cans, sleeping on the sidewalks at night.

"Lecio somehow got his life changed by the love of Jesus. So now he uses his seminary training in a ministry to street kids. He picks them up off the streets and takes them to a Baptist encampment outside the city, an encampment built some years ago with Lottie Moon offering money. They get a bath and get all dressed up. They sing songs and play games and swim in the pool and hear for the very first time in their lives that there is a God who loves them, a God who wants to give them a better life. For Lecio Wanderley, God's call was to see a world bigger than he had ever seen before, right in his own backyard. When we let God take charge of our lives, we can often see a bigger world right where we live."[24]

Communion with Dom Helder Camara

Dom Helder was a small man but towering international icon in ecumenical and secular circles of the 1960s. He was the Archbishop of Recife who stood up to a brutal and deceptive Brazilian Dictatorship and was nominated for the Nobel Peace Prize three times. Dad was an early student of Liberation Theology, and understood Dom Helder to be prophetic, or someone who is speaking truth to power in the present age: "When I feed the poor, they call me a saint, but when I ask why the poor are hungry, they call me a communist." He was thrilled when it was announced that Dom Helder was coming to our *Casa Forte* neighborhood to celebrate communion. He invited me as a father-son didactic opportunity for which I was not eager or prepared. At that time, Southern Baptist MKs had absorbed from their community that Catholic Mass was at best a boring ritual. Nonetheless, I watched as Dad, a North American Southern Baptist missionary, stood in long line with locals to take the Roman Catholic wine and wafer into his body from the hands of Dom Helder Camara. It looked to me like an act of risky defiance of the unspoken missionary rules or just overreaching to impress his neighbors.

It was only much later in Guatemala that I understood it to be a sacred moment in my journey of understanding the bread and

In line for communion with Dom Helder Camara, Jardim Carioca, Casa Forte, Recife.

wine of Christian communion are universal gifts offered to all people without exclusion. Fr Gregory Schaffer, a missionary priest in Guatemala and one of the greats our time, received our *Transformational Journeys*[25] groups and left his profound mark on many of us. He knew I was not Catholic, so I stood in line for communion expecting only a simple blessing. With authority, he pressed a wafer into my palm and placed the chalice under my chin. "Daniel, this the body of Christ and his Blood, take, eat and drink!" I did, thanking my father for preparing me for that transcendent moment that defined so many others.

Saudades

It is the most powerful word in the Portuguese language. *Saudades* is enough nostalgia to bring back tears, laughter, and an overwhelming desire to live the past in the present. It's leaving part of the *coração* (heart) behind. Most expats and missionaries from warm people cultures like Brazil who have spent more than two years overseas undergo an unseen process upon re-entering the United States of America. It's challenging for all, even debilitating for some. "We called ourselves *Bramericanos* (Bramericans). We cried together and laughed together and became closer than our families in the states. That remained right up until the day Dorothy and Glenn were gone. Anyone would tell you that while we are here in the States, our hearts are in Brazil." (Orman Gwynn, Interview, 2017)

It is difficult to describe the deep and abiding sense of Christian communion and growth that was present in the life of Southern Baptist missionaries to Brazil in the second half of the twentieth century. They brought a synchronic mix of sustainable community development projects with funding to back it up. They manifested a fervor for loving the Brazilian people. In Biblical language, it could be described as the caterpillar-to-butterfly emergence of the *beloved community* described in St. Paul's Epistles and later interpreted by Dr. Martin Luther King Jr. "Dr. Martin Luther King's beloved community exhibits agape love, which, as the love of God operating in the human heart, seeks to [preserve and create community]"[26]

The *Povo Brasileiro* (Brazilian people) and their Baptist churches responded with an abiding respect and hunger for what these vibrant and idealistic missioners were bringing. The simplicity and positivity of the message that following Jesus could mean personal transformation was contagious. All of this oxygenated with the heart-and-soul hymn music that fell on open ears that had been dismayed by poverty, the military dictatorship, and the formality of the Catholic liturgies.

It was the dawning of the age of the *Convenção Batista Brasileira*, the Brazilian Baptist Convention, an awakening that kindled the evangelical illumination of the Brazilian culture and faith in the nineteenth and twentieth centuries.

Missionary Bill Ichter (Bill and Jerry Ichter, I.M.B. Missionaries, South Brazil, 1956–1990), before his passing into the light in 2019, released his Memoirs Part 1, that features an intimate and entertaining look at the relationship between the missionaries and the Brazilian Baptists. "When I was commissioned as a missionary of the Board. [I.M.B.], present at the occasion was the renowned evangelist, Dr. Billy Graham. One thing I will never forget is that, after the final prayer, Billy Graham came by to congratulate each one of the newly appointed missionaries. As he stood in front of my wife and I, he said something that has been indelibly engraved in my memory. 'Oh! You are going to Brazil. How I envy you. Brazil is a great country. I would love to spend my whole life preaching the gospel there. Brazil is a great country!" Early in his missionary career, Uncle Bill spoke to the Annual Assembly of the Brazilian Baptist Convention and reflected on the overwhelming truth of Graham's words: "Brazil is really a great country! Why? Is it because our climate is warmer and more agreeable? Is it because our scenery is more beautiful? Or is it because our sky has more stars and our forests have more flowers? No, my dear brothers and sisters, Brazil is a great country because it is inhabited by Brazilians!"[27] Fortuitously, Graham and Uncle Bill shared leadership years later at the *Rio Maracanã* stadium Crusade of 1974.

Graham preached to an estimated six hundred and fifteen thousand people over five days, inspired at each celebration by an eleven thousand five hundred-voice choir directed by Uncle Bill.

The missionaries labored alongside Brazilian leaders as equal partners to inspire the next generation of Brazilian Baptists. They didn't recall exactly how many choir presentations, youth camps or health clinics opened; airlifted patients, radio broadcasts, seminary graduates, or even how many new faith professing Christians joined their churches. What they remembered was the gratitude, the joy, and the authentic transformation of people. The mix of Brazilian melodies pouring out of open windows on cobblestone streets didn't fade until years after their destiny was to say goodbye.

Dad's *saudades*: "Let me be frank to confess to you that one of the things I miss the most from the mission field, from a place where most of the Christians are new Christians, is that sense of excitement, that enthusiasm, that vibrancy that comes from the hearts of those who are new in Christ and still have that enthusiasm about them."[28]

The journey from Recife, Brazil *back* to Arkansas was yanking the chain on some hard-won life habits. For veterans of crossing cultures like Mom and Dad, the Brazilian urbanity they lived in Recife weighs heavily on the unconscious mind that doesn't forget the smells of freshly cut sugar cane, the bus exhaust, or the brilliant colors and dances of *São João* (an exuberant, irreverent mix of the Corn Harvest, St John's day blended with a staged shot gun wedding and intricate square dances.)

Saudades of the close-up hugs and kisses of friendly Brazilian greetings that are suddenly absent. It takes more than a few months back home to appreciate the benefits of no more lines at the bank, central air, and a return of passion for the Arkansas Razorbacks. It never was a sentiment of one culture or country over the other, but rather a place in the heart that yearns for a unity and reconciliation of humanity that can only invade the present in fleeting moments. Sometimes the unexpected encounter with an old friend in an airport comes close

According to Mom, by the time they left Brazil in 1978 Dad had been offered on separate occasions the Presidency of both the São Paulo Baptist Theological Seminary and the Baptist Theological

Seminary of North Brazil (S.T.B.N.B.), where they had served for 13 years. These were family secrets at that time, and my read of it was my dad's saying no to these opportunities was based on a passion for the classroom. I never knew all the reasons why they left what I thought was the best time in the best place on earth for them.

It dawned on me years later that they missed their only son; and my Aunt Glenna Lybrand urgently needed an assist in settling the Hickey family estate. She and her brother had grown closer over the *tesseract* travel years. (A tesseract is an interstellar travel shortcut, more or less, described in *A Wrinkle In Time*, by Madeleine L'Engle.) Dad and Aunt Glenna led lives of frequent travel and shared its delights and disorientation.

The sharp business acumen and enthusiasm of my Grandfather Glenn Hickey was giving way to dementia, and needed immediate attention. Indeed, the first months of my parent's return were spent with Dad and his father sorting through hundreds of IOUs to people in Montgomery County whose need for a small loan matched his dad's big heart. Another painful episode was a Texas lake real estate deal that went further south and had to be liquidated.

After a short search, they were invited to "come in view of a call" to Calvary Baptist in Batesville, in northeast Arkansas. This is a one-day job interview that includes a sermon after which a Baptist church votes yes or no on a candidate for pastor. They voted yes. Dad and Mom were now facing the Carl Jung definition of growth: "In my case, pilgrim's progress consisted in my having to climb down a thousand ladders until I could reach out my hand to the little clod of earth that I am."[29] It was going through the painful lows of giving up Brazil that became the rising again toward their high calling.

Dr. Hickey, the Expository Preacher of Calvary Baptist Church, Batesville, Arkansas

One of Dad's highlights at Calvary Baptist Church occurred when he was absent. The guest preacher was Billy Simmons from Bethlehem Baptist Church. After a rousing concert by the gospel choir, Rev. Billy began his sermon. "By chance that some of y'all did not hear the announcement or read it in your bulletin and you came out here tonight to hear your pastor. As you can see, this is not Brother Hickey. I am slightly darker than he is! I think you have a very wonderful pastor, a man of God, a man that I believe that is a pillar of this community, one that loves his church, loves God, and Brother Jim this is being recorded, isn't it? He may want to hear this before he gives me the five dollars he promised me." Uproarious congregational laughter is registered on the CD recording.[30]

Dad had reveled in getting to preach at Bethlehem Baptist Church hosted by Billy Simmons. He was inspired by the black gospel choirs and preaching, always making a point of church swapping with them. You could count on him to get misty when any recording was played of M.L.K.'s speeches.

A careful listening of his Calvary, Batesville sermons excoriates American cultural Christianity. To sit in the pews was to bear the load of Dad's blunt insights from the Brazilian mission years mixed with the joy of his salvation. He preached passionately about America as Babylon, churches content to do business as usual, and the *alegria* (joy) of union with the transcendent available to all who would give their life without reservation to it. According to his flock in Batesville, that was just what they asked for in a pastor. Dad's time in the Calvary pulpit had transcendent life experiences behind it, and the baritone often played with his words in the freer African American church cadences. "Our church was on a mission, and he was what we wanted, one of the finest preachers and pastors I have ever known. Once he preached himself right off the stage but got up, a little embarrassed, but never missed a beat; that was Glenn." (Larry Davis, member of Calvary Baptist, Batesville, Interviews, 2015, 2018)

Being a pastor and wife can be as awkward a proposition as drinking from the tiny grape juice glasses used in Baptist communion. In practice, very few couples can pull it off with the grace and equilibrium that enables both to express their full human potential over a fifty-year marriage. At the bottom of their formula, Dad practiced equality, and Mom was eager to break with the expectations of the four churches they served together.

They began their co-ministry during seminary in Fort Worth, with two short stints at Eagle Mt. and Corinth Baptist churches. Next up to the Texas panhandle to serve First Baptist Wellington, Texas, then as missionaries to Brazil in separate churches for 14 years. They served together again years later at Calvary Batesville, in Arkansas. According to Mom, they did great together because they had a fourteen-year break in Brazil!

They were all in for gender equality in church and culture and were quick to recommend to friends and colleagues *Women in the World of Jesus*[31] by Frank and Evelyn Stagg. This husband wife team champion the idea that we see played out in the New Testament of Jesus early followers struggling to understand his words: *whoever does the will of God is my mother, and my brother, and my sister,* [Mk. 3:35] and the proclamation that *in Christ there is no male nor female.* [Gal. 3:28]

If there was any doubt about wives publicly submitting to husbands my mom erased it frequently: "Once Glenn surprised Dorothy and the choir with a visit to the choir room minutes before the Christmas cantata. He awkwardly interrupted the rehearsal and asked if she wanted the deacons and himself to enter the sanctuary before or after the choir's entrance. Dorothy responded, 'You can drop down from the ceiling for all I care!' A stunned and giggly silence was followed by Glenn's meek response, 'Well, OK, honey'" (Cathy Davis, member, Calvary Baptist Batesville, Interview, 2015)

Dad had arranged a sabbatical in Little Rock for their dear friends Ademar and Janete Paegle, Brazilian colleagues from Recife days. Ademar Paegle was the visiting chaplain and often introduced in local Baptist churches as "Dr. Paegle and his wife Janete." Knowing that Janete Oliveira had her own career as an accountant for the State of *Pernambuco*, Mom broke protocol to insist on an equal status introduction of Janete Oliveira by the local church leaders.

Southern Baptist Brouhaha

By 1979, the Southern Baptist Convention was the largest Protestant denomination in the United States. They had the most prodigious evangelical missionary-sending organization in the world and held vast networks of influence and power in popular media, culture, politics, and religion. This was all about to shift dramatically. Over the next 20 years, a civil war raged between the conservative and moderate pastors, churches, universities, seminaries, and members of the Southern Baptist network. The communion was irretrievably broken, and the divorce took years of acrimony to subside.

It prompted Dad and Mom's hero Jimmy Carter to declare in October of 2000: "I have finally decided that, after 65 years, I can no longer be associated with the Southern Baptist Convention,' the 76-year-old former president said in a letter mailed to 75,000 Baptists nationwide on Thursday by a group of moderate Texas Baptists. Carter said the Southern Baptist Convention, which has almost 16 million members, has adopted policies 'that violate the basic premises of my Christian faith, including a denominational statement that prohibits women from being pastors and tells wives to be submissive to their husbands.' He said the 'most disturbing' reason he and his wife decided to disassociate themselves from the Southern Baptist Convention was the elimination of language in June that identifies Jesus Christ as 'the criterion by which the Bible is to be interpreted.'"[32]

By now my parents were proficient at the inner and outer adaptation that changing their address demands every four years. Dad received the invitation to interview for the Pulaski Baptist Association Director of Missions job in Little Rock, consulted with Mom, and they were suddenly saying tearful goodbyes and joyful hellos again right on the four-year cycle. Batesville to Little Rock, Arkansas had a unique version of culture shock.

"Glenn and Dorothy stepped smack into the middle of this brouhaha in 1982 when they accepted the position of Director of Missions. Glenn jumped into the hotbed of the Baptist Mafia, and he had to deal with the whole shooting match." (Dr. Clyde Glazener, former Pastor, Calvary Baptist Church, Little Rock, Interview, 2015)

Quietly, Mom and Dad soon followed their conscience and good friends Tom Logue and Clyde Glazener into the Arkansas fold of the Cooperative Baptist Fellowship. They joined Calvary Baptist Church in Little Rock, part of the new moderate movement of former Southern Baptists. Under Clyde's leadership as their Pastor, they found a new spiritual home.

"The 1985 annual meeting was a watershed moment in the conservative revolution in the convention," said Gregory Wills, professor of church history and dean of Southern Baptist Theological Seminary's the school of theology. "Southern Baptist moderates mobilized all their resources to stop the conservative advance at the Dallas meeting. Their bid to regain the presidency failed and Charles Stanley was reelected." (Source—Baptist Press, David Roach)

Dad had strong opinions on the controversy but was known for being a diplomat. His good friend and pastor, Clyde Glazener, was not. They were present together at the 1985 Dallas convention reception shortly after the defining key vote to reelect Charles Stanley as S.B.C. President.

Clyde enjoyed recalling Dad's reaction to his frank expression of opinions after the Dallas vote. "We were at the convention, and Jim Jones came up to me, he was the regional editor of the *Star/Telegram*, and he said, 'Clyde, what do you think of the new president?'

"'Not much!'

"He replied, 'Why is that?'

"'I would have rather had a Baptist.'

"'What do you mean?'

"'Actually, I would rather have had a Methodist to Charles Stanley.'

"'What are you talking about?'

"'Well, he is not a Baptist, he doesn't believe in religious liberty. He is a fundamentalist and just wants to control things.... He just wants to drive the bus, without paying any bills, and his church gives very little to the (Southern Baptist) Convention. So, I would just rather have nearly anybody!'

"'Is that right?' Jim Jones was stunned."

Clyde concluded the story with a mischievous grin that turned to laughter. "I looked around, and Glenn was clear across the room as far away as he could get from me!" (Clyde Glazener, Interview, 2015)

Mom and Dad were at first heartbroken as they lost their community to a civil war under the guise of biblical correctness. This led to the steady erosion of the International Mission Board, the most effective Protestant mission organization of the twentieth century. At the height of the schism, as she heard of the damaging impacts on the Brazilian mission field and to her former colleagues, Mom privately called the group that took over the "damned fundamentalists," to which Dad could only chuckle.

I thought that after Brazil, Arkansas Southern Baptist life for my parents would be incredibly boring. My glamorized title for my dad's Director of Missions job which he held from 1982 to 1995 was "The Baptist Bishop of Little Rock." He became a Pastor to Pastors, the sub preacher, the mission trip leader, and always the cyclist. He blazed every possible route in Central Arkansas, often taking Pastor buddies along who could keep up. Mom reached out to Pastor's wives, hosting events with her disarming, irreverent honestly.

After hearing these testimonials from Baptist leaders in Little Rock, I realized that my parents were still out there living on the edge of joyful uncertainty, in the courageous discipline of reaching out and making themselves vulnerable to fellow pilgrims and strangers. Their destiny was not geography, but the daily choice to be fully present where they were.

"Glenn invented the phrase *Rock Visions* and used it in meetings with the Little Rock mayor, police chief, and other luminaries to keep them in the loop of what the S.B.C. churches were offering the community." (Reverend Don Cooper, Interview, 2017)

Billy White, Pastor of Second Baptist Church in downtown Little Rock during Dad's tenure, said, "Glenn was a Little Rock visionary at a time when the Southern Baptists were focused on control issues. He was a strategic visionary. He had the ability to see the big picture, and loved putting strategy together, but knew to cooperate with God to get there… It wasn't just that he did long-range strategic planning according to some new book, but I remember He went to Habakkuk, Chapter 2:2-4 (The Old Testament Canon).[33] He was a deeply spiritual man who believed in prayer…knowing that we were the hands and feet of Jesus.

"When trying to pull preachers together, oh my goodness, what a challenge! He had a warm pietistic gift but put his strategy forward in a way that people (pastors) could run with it. At the heart of it was fulfilling the Great Commission, honoring Matthew 25:18-20[34] (New Testament Canon) … I loved the fact that he viewed Central Arkansas as his mission field and acted not as denominational worker, or a bureaucrat, but as a missionary (sent) to Little Rock. He showed up on his bike one time. He was quiet about things, that was the kind of guy he was. He would just go ahead and do what he thought was the right thing to do, and you would get to catch up with him." (Billy and Lisa White, Interview, 2016, Billy served as Pastor for 2nd Baptist Church, Little Rock, 1990s).

In 1985, three years into his Pulaski County Missions Director ministry, the fact that Little Rock was almost 50% unchurched got under his missionary skin. At the annual gathering of the ministers of Pulaski Baptist association he declared: "By 1990, unless trends in this city are reversed, Little Rock will become a pagan city with over 50% of its population unchurched…. My vision for Pulaski Baptists is that we will take that challenge as seriously as we expect missionaries in Africa or South America to take it. It is of churches working together in the warm and exciting fellowship of a people who are caught up in excitement of doing God's mission, who leave behind small plans and small ways of thinking about each other."[35]

During these challenging years Dad made it part of his job description to renew himself by organizing several mission trips for

Little Rock churches to serve Baptist missions and build churches in Guatemala and Brazil.

He was the among the first to welcome Dr. Ed Simpson to the Pulaski Association. "In 1990, I became pastor of First Baptist in Sheridan, Arkansas. "Dr. Hickey called me and welcomed me into the Little Rock Pulaski Baptist Association of Arkansas. I appreciated the fact that he had so much wisdom from his years on the mission field. When you are in the role of Missions Director, you are often intervening in churches with deep conflict. Sometimes they're ready to relieve the pastor or other leaders in the church, and probably would if not for someone like Dr. Hickey. He was like a shepherd over the sheep, and we as the pastors were his sheep. I think you need to look at Dr. Hickey as missionary (first). Not everyone can pick up a foreign language as he did. In whatever way God brought opportunities to his door, he seized the moment. He was always reading a good book, and like a many of the professor types, he was always collecting stuff. Every time I heard him say something, I would always leave with an illustration, a word, or some truth that helped me…. He was a mediator between sides of controversies, and his character was such that when he messed up, he was the first to say, 'I'm sorry.'" (Dr. Ed Simpson Interview, 2016) Dr. Ed gave the last gift to my family by presiding over Dad's memorial service and offering testimony to a life well lived.

Reverend Don Cooper, moderator for Dad's retirement luncheon as the Pulaski Director of Missions, observed that Dad carried the Ouachita Barbershop Quartet tradition into his ministry in Little Rock. "Y'all have seen pictures of Glenn singing with the Ouachita quartet. I want to remind you that Glenn has never been a solo singer. He's a harmony man! During his tenure, Glenn did a wonderful job of creating fellowship and harmonizing the churches that were leaning one way or another. He agreed personally with pastors like Randy Hyde of Pulaski Heights and Clyde Glazener of Calvary Baptist in Little Rock. Glenn would have joined them whole hog but never let his personal positions get in the way of cooperating (with all the churches)."

Dr. Ray Higgins, coordinator since 2005 of Cooperative Baptist Fellowship of Arkansas, enjoyed what Dad and Mom brought to the region. "It was Glenn and Dorothy's spirit. They were big tent people, progressive on race relations, and my sense was that they were also progressive on women in ministry. That was just their theological makeup. Glenn, as he moved in the room with people, was quiet, reserved, and dignified. He was kind, compassionate, with a heart for the disadvantaged." (Dr. Ray Higgins Interview, 2016)

OVERFLOW

Dad jumped into extracurricular activities in the Director of Missions, Little Rock years like an eighteen-year old college freshman. He was asked to be a volunteer Ham Radio communications specialist if a major earthquake in the New Madrid fault shook Missouri and Arkansas to pieces. He gladly jumped forward to be trained as a communications first responder. The team was on high alert, except the only time the Arkansas ground shook in those years was the "Calling of the Hogs" sound vibrations on April 4th, 1994, when the University of Arkansas Razorback Men's Basketball team defeated Duke and became the N.C.A.A. National Champions.

Nominated and elected President of the Southern Baptist Conference of Associational Directors of Missions for 1992-1994, he relished most the weeks at Glorieta Baptist Assembly retreat each year in the New Mexico Carson National Forest. He relished least the national newsletter responsibilities every three months.

An invitation came from Dr. Daniel R. Grant, president of O.B.U., to join the Board of Directors at my parents' alma mater. This caught him by surprise. It was a teachable moment for me to see him move from a confessed feeling of inadequacy to his "ten-year-old dreamer" excitement about this new adventure.

Dr. Bernes K. Selph was a generation ahead of Dad at O.B.U., Southwestern Seminary, and in Arkansas pastoral ministry. It was an immense pleasure to interview his early hero, creating the *Bernes Selph Oral*

History Series. "The life story of Bernes K. Selph is an inspiring, heart-warming story of a person overcoming very difficult circumstances to become in the family of Southern Baptists an outstanding scholar, teacher, pastor and denominational statesman." This is an eight-part series of interviews that includes the advent of radio in Dr. Selph's early years:

"The first time I ever heard of radio was from my uncle. One Monday morning early he and grandad were out harnessing the (mule) team. I had gotten up and was out with them, and my uncle was telling us about it and he said, 'You know, yesterday we went (to town) and they had a contraption there, and you would plug it into the batteries, and you can hear music, and you can hear people talking just out of the air! Comes out of the air with no wires, except the wires to the batteries, a little ol' instrument. You know, it won't be long until a fella can't cuss out a mule in the field without everybody hearing him.' For a country boy, that was a real problem!"[36]

Dad also escaped for frequent thirty mile plus bike rides all over central Arkansas, braving dogs and pick-up trucks before the era of extensive cycling lanes and trails. When he was 58 he broke his wrist trying to learn to snow ski at Snow Creek, Missouri. He persisted and five years later enjoyed skiing with his grandchildren in Breckenridge, Colorado. My theory on Dad's capacity for a high state of *flow*[37] is that he prepared well for these activities, and they also involved travel, which created an overflow of *alegria*.

"Do I Still Have the **Folego** (Mojo)?"

At sixty-nine, Dad chose to spend the dawn of a new millennium with our *Transformational Journeys* team in Recife, leading some Kansas City mission trippers into mutual service projects with Brazilians in his *lugares do coração* (places of the heart). *Transformational Journeys*, a volunteer mission travel company based in Kansas City, was founded by the author.

"I began this trip wondering if I could do it again, be an effective witness and proclaimer of God's good news to lost mankind. I immediately was hit with the difficulty of my task in facing seventeen-degree snowstorm conditions in Kansas City for our departure. The storm seemed to be closing in on the way to the airport, but just as quickly the storm moved out and our runways were clear for departure. Good memories began to flood my inner being as the plane approached Recife, looking down to *Praia de Gaibu*, *Rio Jaboatão*, and *Praia de Candeias*. The time Dan and I rode our bikes to a place near *Gaibu* and learned how futile it is to ride thin-tired road bikes onto the loose sand of beach roads; vacation times at the old beach house in *Piedade*, and the famous *Jangada* fishing expedition with Fred Spann, Norton Lages, and Wade Smith. (Wade and Shirley Smith, I.M.B. Missionaries, North Brazil, 1962–1980) These *Doces Recordações* (sweet memories) soon gave way to the reality of ninety-four-degree climate of the Recife summer.

Reunion Day with IBCI members. There were Muitos abraços!

"Ibura Homecoming! What an emotional experience to enter a new, large temple and see a five hundred plus crowd gathered to ring in the new year together. As I sat there taking in the service and greeting old friends, I could not help but think of Jesus' parable of the mustard seed and how the seed planted nearly thirty years ago with a small struggling congregation of sixty people. The service started around 10 p.m. and ended shortly after midnight. It included twenty-four baptisms, a celebration of the Lord's Supper, and installation of church officers for the new year. One of the most touching moments came when the deacon body was called forward to serve the supper: There were four deaconesses and five deacons, all of whom I had ordained. After all this, in true Brazilian style, there was a *Festa de Confraternização* (A raucous fellowship party)! I only got back to the compound at 2 a.m.!

"The first preaching gig for the next day was at *Campo Grande*, a church in a *bairro popular* (working class neighborhood). The service was very *animada*, (lively guitars, percussion, and high volumes of congregational singing). We brought renowned artist and composer Mark Hayes who took over the keyboards and gifted flautist Terry Lois Gregory who with the young congregation really lifted the rafters and got them into all the body movement appropriate to the up-tempo music. In another unexpected moment, the music director, *Ronildo*, was the son of one of my former students. This relaxed atmosphere gave me complete freedom in preaching. Temps were in the 90s and so was the humidity, and I had worn a coat and tie. Noting the informality of the setting, I began by saying, "Considering the heat outside and spiritual warmth of this service, this coat seems quite inappropriate, so excuse me while I free myself from it.' I then removed my coat and tossed it over on the pulpit chair. This brought the house down. I was told later that Pentecostal preachers often throw their coats into the audience. I cannot describe the freedom I suddenly felt again in the Portuguese language. I used a complete manuscript for the sermon titled, 'What the spirit is saying to the churches,' but did not feel at all bound to it. It was an exhilarating experience." (Glenn Hickey *Transformational Journeys* Journal, 2000)

The Funder for Founders

On this same voyage, Dad also met Recife neighborhood legend Moab Silva:

"I met Pastor Glenn when I was invited to cook for the *Transformational Journeys* group of American visitors. At that time, I was developing a few activities for the children from the *favela* (shantytown slum where most homes are improvised) that was close to my home. Since the children were always in my home, Pastor Glenn and the group wanted to know more about them and visit their homes and families. Our group did not even have a name yet but was being recognized and valued by Pastor Glenn. He had a clinical eye and specific suggestions. It was not just a bunch of poor kids to him, but people who needed an opportunity. He began to generously send monthly funds with a request—'It's for the children to run and play.' Indeed, these funds gave us the conditions to rent a sports gym for our recreation. Our friendship deepened, and by July we founded the 'Friends Forever Christian Community.'" (Moab Silva, Founder of Friends Forever based in Recife, Brazil)

The Folego⁺ Filled Amazon Guide

After the exhaustive Recife days, Dad was slated to lead the *Transformational Journeys* trip extension to an Amazon River resort, a cushy way to recover from an arduous mission trip. Not to be. His destiny was to rise to the high calling of becoming a *Guia desenrolado* (Master tour guide having what it takes to untangle complex challenges).

We trusted the pre-trip planning to the locals in Manaus and sent a group who paid pricier for the expectation of basic creature comforts and at least a three-star B&B on the river of legends. It was an unbearably long ride from the Manaus airport in the *Volkswagen Kombi* to this paradise lost, and the group grew increasingly restless as dawn approached. At last they saw a gate with a potbellied gatekeeper in a downsized *sunga*.

"*Oi, é o Senhor Glenn?*" (Hello, are you Mr. Glenn?)

This brought incredible relief among the bedraggled travelers as Glenn and the greeter chatted it up. They were then presented with deplorable sagging, moldy beds, a leaky roof, naked top toilets, and a dangerous fire escape staircase to get to their exalted rooms. They were facing quarters three stars below their expectations. This marvel was not on any booking.com site and never would be. This became a serious crisis for Dad since he represented *Transformational Journeys* and was basically caught in less than a *SUNGA* as to explain this vastly oversold *Journeys* destination. His humor, creativity, and power of persuasion were animated, and his legend grew. The Amazon waters flooding over the group morale were turned to expensive wine as much was made of this upscale camping opportunity. With Dad's urging, the hotel staff quickly became overachievers, carting fancy furniture up the stairs at risk to their own safety and serving gourmet local fish delicacies in the evenings.

All of Dad's nuanced interpreting skills and adrenalin flowed as he delivered news of the absence of the return driver, with a hasty exit to beg for a cell phone from two riverside lovers. He saved the dignity of more than the moment and was successful at asking for the only phone for 100 miles and getting the group out of this debacle. Everyone was deliriously delighted that they had survived the jungle with a panache unavailable to ordinary mortals.

Veterans of the Journey to the Amazon *Pousada dos Dolphinos* (The Pink Dolphin's B&B) Alexandra Moschell Terrill, David Lowe, and Denise Di Piazzo unanimously concurred that it was Dad's *Dar um Jeito* (improvisational skills), humor, and boundless optimism that morphed a disaster into a lifetime treasured memory.

Folego/Mojo—or astonishing bursts of endurance in a long ordeal.

Preacher's Kid Sermon Reviews

Preacher's kids are only one step away from the agony of missionary kids, who must endure their parents' sermons in two languages. Missionary kids, by virtue of their youth, learn the new language and culture much faster than their parents. Brazilian MKs endured a few sermons in bad Portuguese, but time enabled most of us to see the illumination in our parent's efforts. Here are Dr. Glenn Hickey's best pulpit moments in the opinion of his son, who stayed awake during most of his preaching and eventually took to heart his cause.

The Good Samaritan Shows Up Early

When he was thirty-two, Dad challenged the faithful at First Baptist Wellington, Texas with his take on the Parable of the Good Samaritan. "I read an interesting article once on the story of the Good Samaritan entitled, 'Suppose the Good Samaritan Had Arrived Earlier.' The writer suggested that Christians need to consider what the Good Samaritan would have done if he had arrived while this man was being attacked. He might have simply done nothing. He might have merely sat down at a safe distance and watched this scene as the Romans once watched the gladiatorial battles with cold detachment…. Or, He might have waited until the fight was over and the danger was past and then jumped in to do his Red Cross service, like many Christians who want to do good so long as it doesn't cost them anything and no danger is involved.

"But I don't believe the Good Samaritan that Jesus told about would do these things. I believe he would have been in the fight, fighting for the good and the right, doing his best to help a man in danger and in need."[38]

Measuring our Christianity by Don'ts

My only memory of my great grandmother Hickey was the unique mix of spitting snuff into a large urn and her frequent use of holy language. My opinion was filtered through my mom, who was mortified by her behavior. My dad's lifetime witness to her was more thorough:

"I always think of my grandmother as a very devout woman. I know she had lots of positives in her life. I saw them. But when we were young children growing up, we saw mostly the negatives in my grandmother's Christian life. She had a long list of things you couldn't do on Sunday, and we had heard them all. You can't go swimming on Sunday, can't play ball, can't play hopscotch, can't play marbles, and on and on. She had a list of those things. I remember one time we were all at Grandmother's house on Sunday, all the grandkids together there, and we had run out of something to do that Sunday afternoon. One of my cousins finally got exasperated and said, 'Grandma, is there anything you can do on Sunday besides go to church?'

"You can't build your Christian life on things you don't do. Because if all you have is the Ten Commandments, pretty soon you won't have them because you won't be able to keep them without positive power."[39]

Nothing Succeeds like Failure

A foreign mission field like Brazil soon tests the character of the best men and women. To be successful as long-term missioners, they had to master a new language and new habits of thought and action that demand a decisive goodbye to many North American habits and expectations. For example, handshake greetings are replaced by hugs for men and kisses on the cheek for women. As they presented their best selves to the new culture, their shortcomings were quickly exposed to their peers and the Brazilian nationals. Reservoirs of grace toward each other and a deep sense of humor usually prevailed. Failures were inevitable and became teachable moments as they struggled to grow into their *lado brasileiro* (Brazilian selves).

"Simon Peter was gifted with the gift of failure. There are examples of his failure:

"Peter has doubts and fails to walk on the water.

"'Lord, if it's you,' Peter replied, 'tell me to come to you on the water.'

"'Come.'

"Then Peter got down out of the boat, walked on the water, and came toward Jesus. But when he saw the wind, he was afraid and, beginning to sink, cried out, 'Lord, save me!' Immediately Jesus reached out his hand and caught him. 'You of little faith, why did you doubt?' (Matt 26:28-31 N.I.V.)

"The Bible is full of men who were failures: Noah, Jacob, Moses, David, Jonah, Elijah, Matthew, Thomas, and the greatest of all, Simon Peter. 'Nothing succeeds like success.' I take exception to

that! Maybe there are a few people in life who never failed at anything, always did the right thing, made the right choices, never
made a mistake, and always came out on top in the climb up the
ladder of success, but have you ever known one? I have known
people who started out successful and ended up failures. They felt
they could never stumble or fall. I have also seen many who failed
in life and kept coming back until they became successful. So, from
what I have seen, a better proverb to say might be, 'Nothing succeeds like failure!'"[40]

Making Friends with the Bible

"It is, I believe, a helpful approach to scripture to see the sixty-
six books of the Bible as though they were persons out there in the
vast world of our…experience. Some of these sixty-six potential
friends are barely known by name. I must admit, Leviticus and I
barely know each other. I would not list the book of Numbers among
my closest of friends. There may be a time ahead in my spiritual pilgrimage when we will need to get better acquainted, but up until now
we have only spoken to each other occasionally.

"I must admit that as a New Testament professor, there was a time
when Hebrews and I were not very well acquainted. I knew his history and background and could describe him fairly well to my seminary students, but we were not the best of friends. I saw him as a
rather dull and boring type, legalistic and pedantic, given to long and
repetitious monologues on ritual and sacrifice and priestly talk about
things that I had little interest in. Since then, Hebrews and I have
become the best of friends. It happened in 1974, when I was chosen
as the preacher for the annual sermon at our state Baptist convention
in Recife, Brazil. My message for that occasion was taken from the
great missionary passages of Hebrews. The central message of the
book is found in the opening statement, 'God has spoken to us in a
son', or to say it literally, 'God has spoken in sonship.' He has spoken
in a way that is new and infinitely more profound. The emphasis here

is on the way that God has spoken. God has communicated himself to us through the person of his son.

"Hebrews was prepared as a sermon to a congregation, probably in the seventh decade of the first century that was in danger of missing the boat in relation to God's redemptive mission in the world. The verb used in chapter 2, verse 1 is a nautical term. It literally means to drift or float alongside. It carries the idea of a river flowing past a given point, or a ship slipping from its anchorage and drifting away. The peculiar thing about the verb, however, is that it appeared in the passive rather than the active voice. It is not saying that our danger as a congregation of God's people is that of drifting away ourselves. Our danger is being drifted by. In other words, we are the stationary object, and something else is moving and is about to pass us by."[41]

Christian Communing

Mom and Dad experienced the beloved community or *koinonia* in the form of their day-to-day life with missionary colleagues in the *Campinas* language school. Imagine a *Novela* (Brazilian soap opera) where every day there is a new drama, even if it's only to learn how to say *torta* instead of pie. This was the legendary story of missionary Marlene Boswell, when during language school in *Campinas*, she received an unexpected visit from a Brazilian family. She was cooking a sumptuous apple pie and was able to communicate effectively the cooking part to the visitors. Pie pronounced in Portuguese is *Pai*, or father. In her best Portuguese she asked them to wait at the front door while she finished putting her father in the hot oven. When she returned to the door to invite them in, they were gone, convinced this missionary was *louca* (crazy). Stories like this were daily in the midst of a shared life in a land of constant delights and just enough perils to keep them living fully each day with one another.

"One of the most interesting and frequent phrases in the New Testament is one-another, the reciprocal pronoun that links two lives together in a mutual relationship. The New Testament speaks of so many ways our lives are to be linked together in Christ in *Koinonia*, in Christian togetherness. We are called to pray for one another, to love one another, to exhort one another, to comfort one another, to bear one another's burdens, to admonish one another, to be of the same mind one toward another, to receive one another, to salute one another, to serve one another, on and on we could go. This is the task of the church, to be a community of love where we belong to each other and encourage one another and stimulate one another toward Christian maturity. In a world that is cold and harsh and impersonal and uncaring, the church should be a haven of caring and understanding. But you and I know that church so much of the time is not this kind of experience."[42]

Listening to Your Partner

Dad was capable of selective hearing and occasionally would tune out primordial people in his life. Here is his confession inside a sermon:

"James is giving us a principle of communication when he says let everyman (every husband and wife) 'be quick to hear.' The gift of understanding, or hearing, of really listening to someone. Have you ever been guilty of this? Your wife is going full out, and she is talking about something that is important to her, and you are not paying any attention and all at once in the middle of all that something comes out that catches your mind and you think 'Hey. I want to know what this is all about' and you decide to actually listen.

"'What did you say?'

"Boy, I don't know what happens in your home, but I know what happens in my home because when I haven't been listening as I should have been, you really hear it then…

"We all need to learn how to listen better, and it begins by shutting the mouth and putting the ear in gear."[43]

Whatever Happened to Mutual Submission?

I never saw my parents assume that their long and fruitful union was anything more than a God-given gift that they could not explain. I did see them mourn with those who were heartbroken and rejoice with folks who had found their bliss. Late in their ministry, they were also keen on affirming both singles and marrieds as blessed estates. If they had a secret, it was a mutuality of submitting to the other's wishes, often quite publicly.

"Ephesians 21 Submit to one another out of reverence for Christ.'

"Ephesians 22 'Wives, submit yourselves to your own husbands as you do to the Lord.'"

"Submit appears only in verse 21, but is to be understood and implied in verse 22. So, we must keep these verses together, we must think about the attitude of mutual submission one to another, the kind of humility we should practice toward each other in the Christian life. Perhaps the best way to explain it is that we as Christians should learn to give way to each other, we must learn to yield the right of way to the other person all along life's journey. That's the basic principle that's involved here. It is the way of Christ, who gave himself up for us, it is the way that Christ taught us when he taught that the greatest of you should be the servant of all. That he who loses his life shall truly find it. This is the basic principle that should permeate all our Christian life. And we should practice it everywhere—Men toward women, women toward men, the old toward the young, and the young toward the old. All of us should learn to yield the right of way to each other along the pathway of life."[44]

Preaching Excessively on the "Sower and Seed"

Dad was a farm boy. He and his sis Glenna had stepped in plenty of cow poop, shucked thousands of corn ears, fed a million chickens, and enjoyed the sweet scent of honeysuckle during their breaks from clearing hundreds of glamorous Arkansas rocks for planting potatoes.

Oden and Mount Ida are in Montgomery County, Arkansas, which is still a national pilgrimage site hallowed for its quartz. So, yes, very glamorous rocks!

"It is instructive to notice how much attention Jesus gave to those who were engaged in the ordinary tasks that support and sustain life in that first century world. The farmers, the fishermen, the orchard keepers—there seems to have been a great deal more interest in these occupations than we have today.

"My wife Dorothy asked me 'Are you going to preach on the seeds again?'

"'Well, yes, since there are lots of parables about the seed and the sower.'

"People of that day were a lot more interested in how a fellow's crops were doing, and that is true in any subsistence society like that of first-century world. You and I live in a society that is characterized by abundance, but we need to realize it is a diminishing abundance, and maybe the time is coming when you and I also will be more directly connected with the land and those who till the soil and are responsible for placing food upon our table." [45]

Adversaries Inside the Church

"I had a good professor friend and pastor friend in Brazil who talked about this often. He said that through the many years of his pastorates he always had at least one or two adversaries in every church he pastored. 'I learned to thank God for my adversaries. I realized along the course of my ministries that even my adversaries, those who were against me, were a blessing to my life, and I realized that somehow God even used them, and they helped me stay on my toes, they made me work harder, and plan harder. Even though they were my adversaries, they contributed something to me, and I am indebted to them.'"[46]

I do remember a generational intolerance toward any sign of laziness manifested in my dad by a knock on the door at 8 a.m. if my room was still silent. Compared to the early-morning drills inflicted on my dad by my grandfather, I had it good!

"I was reared in a family very conscious of time, very intolerant of laziness, or any sign of it. I suppose a part of it was the mentality of those war years. I grew up in that period of WW II when we were all geared to the war effort, to contribute the maximum production of every element of society. In those years, I was a farm boy growing up on a small farm, and my family also had a country store, and as if that were not enough, in the summertime we did custom hay bailing for other people. There was something for everyone to do every hour of the day. My father rose at the crack of dawn, and he could not tolerate anyone sleeping 10 minutes after he himself got up. I remember that very clearly. I would awaken to a recitation of all the things that had to be done that day. Those were the years of production quotas, and we had them on that farm. There was something for everyone to do, and even as small children, my sister and I had it drilled into us the importance of everybody putting in their maximum effort to win the war against the Axis powers.

"I shall never forget. I remember it as if it was yesterday—the resonant voice of Lowell Thomas on the radio announcing the bombing of Pearl Harbor and how that one piece of news galvanized us into a course of action, the total mobilization of all the American people. I believe that is what Paul is calling the church to do here in these verses. The Apostle Paul is advocating this in the thirteenth chapter of Romans. He is talking about waking-up time. Paul is calling the church to do that in these verses. In view of the coming day of judgment and salvation, the church must wake up, and we must set our spiritual time clock to the advancing time clock of God, for time is rapidly running out for us to accomplish our mission in the world.

"Why is the gospel of Jesus Christ not winning the world today as it ought to? Why are we not reaching out beyond our own families and our own people into the lost world out there? I believe the answer lies right here. We haven't set our clocks up. We haven't synchronized our lives to the heartbeat of God as we look out before a lost world."[47]

MOTHERHOOD

Dad and Aunt Glenna's affection for my Grandma Lula was akin to sons and daughters in Brazil who take out huge roadside billboards declaring their mom the best on Mother's Day. They were just more discreet, sending her amazing cards and doting on her when she allowed it.

"Our mother did a lot of little things with love and devotion. It was bathing babies in a number two washtub, laughing and playing and splashing water over us, as two young children. Motherhood was

Glenn and Lula Hickey's 50th wedding anniversary, 1979. (From left) Bob and Glenna Lybrand, Glenn and Lula Hickey, Glenn and Dorothy Hickey.

pasting pictures on the bottom of milk glasses that she cut out of magazines so we would drink all of our milk and have good teeth. Motherhood was inventing little games played while shucking corn so that the task did not seem so long and tedious. Motherhood was putting up with us while we bungled our efforts to plant a spring garden so that she might have the opportunity to talk to us about how God makes things grow. I could go on and on in these memories of what Mother means to me.

"We blame all the problems of the home today on the mothers because they are working and not at home. So many fathers don't realize that half of parenting is fathering."[48]

Characteristics of a Great Person

Dad practiced this habit of finding and serving the "least of these" (Matthew 25:40, NIV) because we noticed that in many a non-public moments he was focused on seeking out the stranger or whoever was least valued in the community.

"Have never known very many great men in my time. I have known a few men that I considered great, and there is a characteristic about great men that I have observed—that in a crowd a truly great man will seek to give attention to the little people, the seemingly insignificant, unnoticed people, in any group gathered about him. One of the men I considered to be a great man was Dr. J. Howard Williams, president of Southwestern Seminary, during our years there, a very kind, gracious and humble man, and yet a great leader and great man of God. I always observed this about him. He made a point in any group of people gathered together to give attention to everyone, especially someone considered rather insignificant that no one else would pay attention to. He seemed to take some extra time to give attention to that person."[49]

Living and proclaiming the present Reign of God received much more airtime than heaven and hell in Dad's teaching and preaching. This was parallel in his mind to the print that living in the present kingdom of God received compared to a future heaven and hell in the New Testament words of Jesus.

"Some people tell me they do not believe in hell. How could you not believe in hell when you see it all around you, when examples of it are before our eyes—things so horrible and terrible we do not like to think about them. I read the newspaper, and sometimes I slam the newspaper shut it's so terrifying."[50]

He preached his most comprehensive sermon on heaven to residents at Parkway Village Health Center in 2005. This group of seniors was attentive regarding their afterlife alternatives. "In that perfect fellowship, we will be able to ask God the answer to some of those baffling questions that we never got the answer to on earth. I will probably ask, 'God, why did our first little baby girl, Debbie, have to die, with only three days of life on earth?' (Mom and Dad lost my sister Debbie in December of 1954, most likely to breathing apnea due to prematurity.) You may ask, 'God, why did I have to suffer so long before I came to this place?' or 'Why did my spouse have to leave me so long ago, and leave me on earth all alone?'

"A class of third graders in Union City, Tennessee was asked the question 'What is heaven like?' How would you answer that? Well, they had their own ways of answering. One little girl who seemed to be unusually romantic for a nine year old said, 'Heaven is where I will meet the man of my dreams.' A little boy was very diplomatic, he ought to end up in politics. 'Heaven is where some very nice teachers and a nice principal will be found.' Another child wrote, 'Heaven is where you will get everything you want, but if you want everything you might not go there.' I thought this was the best one. 'Heaven should be the happiest part of my dead life.'

"Well, you see you can't describe (Heaven), can you?"[51]

Perspective

The astonishing privilege of a son in rural Arkansas in 1940 to be able to soar high above his native landscape in a piper cub aircraft for a new vision of the world was not lost on my father. "I shall never forget when I was a child about nine or ten years old, my first airplane ride. It was a Piper Cub, barely room for two people, and it was County Fair time in Montgomery County and this barnstorming pilot had come to that part of Arkansas. My dad was just about as excited as everyone else. We got in line there, and he got his two dollars out, and it came our turn. He handed the money to the pilot, who stuffed us into the back seat of that piper cub, and we took off. I remember so well it was the Frank Davidson farm, one of the biggest hay pastures in that part of the country, and my family and I had just cut and bailed all the hay on that big field a week before. I will never forget getting up there about eight hundred feet and seeing all that farm laid out below and remarking to my dad, 'Look, Dad, you can see the whole Frank Davidson Farm!'

"I had another experience just this past January, quite a contrast to that, when we were coming back from our trip to Israel, and we boarded a Boeing 747 out of Athens, Greece, and about an hour-and-a-half later, we were forty thousand feet high, passing over northern Yugoslavia, bordering on Austria. It was about the middle of a bright sunny day, and I looked out the left window of that 747, and there was a spectacular panorama before my eyes. The beautiful snow-capped Alps, in all of their splendor, stretching from the eastern edge of Austria, all across Switzerland and into northern Italy and over into the edge of France; you could see them all. A glorious sight.

"What you see depends on your perspective. Our NASA scientists this week, through the marvel of modern radio and space technology, have been able to stand, as it were, on the edge of our solar system. You and I have participated with them in that spectacular view of Saturn, and we have been amazed at what we have been able to see from the perspective of distant space. But none of this, dear friends, is worthy to compare with what the Apostle John saw that day from the tiny Isle of Patmos as God opened the door of Heaven for his servant and let him stand there at the portals and see it all in the glorious, marvelous perspective of eternity."[52]

The Power of Words

The *Seminario Teologico Batista do Norte do Brasil* (North Brazil Baptist Theological Seminary) sits under a grove of mango trees on the *Rua do Padre Ingles*, (the Street of the English Priest). Students didn't mind being interrupted with ripe, rose-colored mangoes falling toward their heads between December and February. There was also an overused ping pong table in the student lounge beneath the classrooms. Between classes there was a loud harmony of student joviality in the vowel-based Portuguese, the sharp rustle of leaves as mangoes rocketed through, and the eternal ping pong notes. This was where Dad became a polyglot theology professor, learning to dance from English to Greek to Portuguese in a perfecting harmony.

"Words have enormous power, and one of the greatest powers of words is found in the words of the teacher. The role of a teacher brings a multiplying effect on the power of our words. When I began my teaching career at the North Brazil Seminary in Recife, Brazil, I was a newly trained Portuguese speaker. They told me I had done well in language school, but I was totally unconvinced of that when I stood to speak my first words in that New Testament class. They were words I carefully chose and placed on the paper of the manuscript from which I read. I started haltingly, but as the days moved along, I slowly gained some measure of certainty. And the thing that prodded me most was watching the students actually taking notes of what I said. By the second semester, some were staying moments after class to ask me a question or add some further thoughts to what I had said. Finally, by the end of that first year, I was hooked on the ministry of teaching, although it did take me a bit longer to get used to teaching Greek in the Portuguese language. Finally, I had become in their eyes a true Professor or Doctor of Theology. And by the end of the second year on the seminary faculty, I could hardly believe it when the students selected me as *Paraninfo*, the equivalent to Professor of the Year. What a great privilege had been given to me to be a teacher. But what a great responsibility also."[53]

The Rhythm of Life

Missionaries on furlough back home are not on vacation. They are in a whirl of explaining their ministries to local churches that fund them. They often faced the discomfort of justifying their labor overseas in a manner beyond the cold numbers of churches planted or students taught in a mystical endeavor that really could only be explained in stories. Mom and Dad's first furlough was a discipline of learning how to accept walking, running, and soaring. They later reminisced that so much had changed between 1964 and 1969 in the United States that it was like visiting a foreign country.

"There was a time in my life that I tried to claim more from this promise than perhaps God intended. I used to think God was saying, 'Child of mine, when you want to soar with wings of an eagle, just wait on me, trust my strength, and I'll make you soar. When you want to run and not be weary, just trust in me, and I'll make you run, and when you want to walk, I'll help you walk and faint not.' Through the difficult experience of a fellow minister and his deep understanding of how God was working in his life through that experience, I came to see this promise of God in a new way.

"We were in Louisville, Kentucky in 1969 for our first furlough on the campus of Southern Seminary. At that time, John Claypool was pastor of Crescent Hill Baptist church near the seminary campus. Some of you may have read his book and know the story of their young daughter, Laura Lue, and her long struggle with leukemia. Toward the last days of Laura's life, John Claypool preached a sermon on this text. He called it 'strength not to faint.' He confessed to his congregation in the midst of that experience, 'I'm not running like the footman, just barely walking through this time, but somehow, God is giving me strength not to faint.'

"Out of that message I learned something that enabled me to go back to Brazil and face my task with new understanding of what it means to live what I would call the God-directed life. I learned that God does not promise to make me soar when I want to or run when I want to or walk when I want to. I learned from this fellow minister that in many of my experiences in Brazil, God exercises his lordship not only over the time and power in my life, but over the rhythm or the pace of my life."[54]

Is the Will of God a Joy or a Burden?

"Life, liberty, and the pursuit of happiness" are key words in the American Declaration of Independence. Is the pursuit of happiness compatible with Christian surrender to a higher calling? This question was thrown in Dad's face on the day of his surrender to Christian ministry in 1950.

"Some people seem to understand the will of God as being a burden to be endured rather than delight of life to be enjoyed. I remember when I sensed God was calling me to the ministry and in a Sunday morning service, I surrendered my life to do the will of God, and to give myself to the Gospel ministry. After that service, I stood down at the front as people came by to shake my hand. I'll never forget the attitude of some people. Why, some people looked like they were attending my funeral. They looked at me like they were looking in a casket at my dead form there, and they would say. 'Oh, I am so happy that you have surrendered to do the will of God,' and shake their head as though it was the worst thing that could happen to me. They weren't glad about it. The only thing they were glad about is that it was me and not them who had to do the will of God.

"Is that what the will of God is? No, the will of God is not some burden to be borne. It is a delight of life. It is a joy to find all that God has for us in life. We must give all of us there is to give in surrender to him. You see, the problem with many of us is we have just enough Christianity to make us miserable and not enough to make us happy."[55]

It was the quite disconcerting to some of us as first-year seminarians at Midwestern Theological Baptist Seminary in early the 1980s, in Kansas City, the idea that the New Testament comes from oral stories originally intended for specific communities in first-century cultures. The dance of rigorous critical analysis of texts using modern scientific tools and the mystical PALAVRAS (words) handed down to us can be threatening or enlightening. The discovery that the synoptic gospels[56] Matthew, Mark, and Luke present a different view of Jesus than the Gospel of John is challenging. Some prefer not to be placed in this tension between how the Bible came to us through human voices and hands over time and the *mysterium tremendum*[57] of how it inspires us in the here and now.

The harmony of science and faith in the practice of Biblical textual interpretation was a delightful struggle that Dad embraced with passion. He agreed heartily with St Augustine and St. Anselm, that as Christians we are to act in "Faith seeking Intelligence." He grasped that the Greek texts were actually written sixty to ninety years after the events in the life of Jesus, and dependent on the oral tradition, or the "story of the storytellers."[58] His labor was to open a channel for moderns to see, hear, and touch the sacred mystery in the ancient texts. The song applies to him" "This little light of mine, I'm gonna let it shine!"

He started by trusting his listeners with the language tools to become interpreters of texts. He always preferred the dialectic approach, bravely leading folks into the wilderness of biblical languages and original cultures. He wandered deep into how the manuscripts were written, trusting his listeners to hear and interpret his words just as the canonical writers had to trust their oral sources and the contributions of the communities for which their stories were intended.

He enjoyed introducing new words to his church listeners. "Abraham's salvation is based on faith, or trust. He exercised faith in God, just like anyone else who is a Christian today. Interesting the way Paul expresses it here. There is no way to translate that into English, but let's make up a word. Literally we would say that he *faithed* God. We don't have a word like that do we? Well, we do have one now. I just used it. We've got it. He *faithed*—He put his trust in God. Abraham then is the father of all who trust in God and look to him for their salvation."

"And we know that in all things God works for the good of those who love him, who have been called according to his purpose." (Romans 8:28, N.I.V.)

"'Works for the good.' This is a very interesting word that is used in the Greek. The word is actually a single compound verb, meaning working together, and we have an English word that when translated directly from the Greek, it's the word *synergism*. It has two components. The first is a preposition, *syn*, which means 'with', and the second part is the word *ergomai*, which is translated 'to work'. So it literally means 'working together' or 'working with.' The word synergism is the cooperative action of two substances, organs, or organisms to achieve an effect of which each is individually incapable."[59]

WALKING THROUGH THE VALLEY OF THE SHADOW

This sermon was first preached in 1981. More than twenty years later, assisting in the caretaking of my mom during her long struggle with Alzheimer's, I often woke up at 5 A.M. hearing the faint voice of my dad reciting Psalm 23 in the living room.

"One of the things we should always remember about this stage of faith is that this pathway is not a detour in our Christian pilgrimage. Nor does it mean we have taken a wrong road somewhere, but rather this is a part of the journey, to walk with Jesus the good shepherd through the valley and in the dark shadows. Many Christians do not understand that. They expect the Christian life to be a bed of roses.

"This was a point that we had to deal with in Brazil as we had many young people who would come to Christ and become Christians with no background whatsoever, and no encouragement whatsoever from their families at home. And many of them came into the Christian faith with very idealistic notions about what the Christian life was to be. I found that I needed to counsel with them in that first moment when they walked into the valley of the shadow and life became difficult. Some of them would say, 'pastor, what have I done wrong? Where have I missed the boat? Have I missed a turn somewhere in the road, because now it's difficult and I thought being a Christian would not be this way?' Then it would be necessary to explain this is not a wrong turn, this is not a detour. This is rather a time of testing when faith is strengthened through trials and difficulty. Yes, the valleys and the shadows are a part of the journey!"[60]

Interpreting the Book of Revelation

A source of great dismay for Dad after his seminary days were the short-sighted and convenient interpretations of the book of Revelation. The idea that the world is ending soon, and so any actions to care for God's precious creation, or reach out to lost humanity, are beside the point. This drove him to intense right-ness indignation.

"Now we are told that when all this happened that John saw this vision, that He saw the great angel, standing there, that there was a voice that roared as a lion, the voice of seven thunders that uttered their voices in verse three. And John said just like when he heard the voices of the seven thunders, just like he recorded the vision of the seven candlesticks, the vision of the seven seals, and the vision of the seven trumpets, he was ready to write what the seven thunders were saying, and the message came to him, to seal it up, and to not write what the seven thunders uttered"…now *what does that mean?* I believe this is simply saying to us that we shall never be able to know and to understand and explain everything that happens on the face of this earth. Some things are beyond our power to comprehend…it is not given to us to understand everything.

"I wish some preachers of the book of Revelation would read that and ponder on it. Some of them seem to think they know everything! They tell you exactly what is going to happen with the armies of the Near East, and the conflict between Iran and Iraq, and the Russian armies now gathering and encircling the land of Poland. They find it in some obscure verse there in the Bible. Some of them even write books about it. I think Hal Lindsey's books are like that. He writes a book and sells millions of them, and when all that doesn't happen exactly like he wrote it, he just writes another book. He sells you another book, and it starts all over again. The mystery of the seven thunders, we cannot know everything."[61]

WHAT I WANT FOR CHRISTMAS

Outside of the churches, Christmas in Brazil was not a big deal in the 1960s and '70s. Artificial Christmas trees were creeping into the stores, but American expats in Recife just 557 miles below the Equator were toasty, schools were out for summer vacation, and the Brazilian public cultural enthusiasm was already centered on *Carnaval* (Mardi Gras) a month later. Missionaries were severely

Dorothy, Dan, and Glenn at Christmas, 1973

tested in their capacity to produce the mystique of Christmas for themselves and their children.

"What do I want most for Christmas? I would like to have more of the enthusiasm that the shepherds found in telling others about Jesus. The scripture says that when the angels announced it, the shepherds lost no time in getting to where the Christ child was born. *They came with haste.*

"The original word means literally 'they came jumping the fences along the way.' You've got to see the fences in Palestine to understand that these were little rock fences, where they piled the rocks up. They are endless, dividing property into very small portions. You can just see those shepherds jumping over those rock fences in a hurry to get to where Jesus was born. I have a feeling that with same sense of urgency they returned to share the good news, to tell everyone everywhere what they had seen. They could not wait to bear witness of the Christ child that they found in Bethlehem's manger."[62]

Keeping the Dream Alive

I believe dreaming new dreams was Dad's secret to joy. At least once a decade, he would dream new dreams and spend enormous amounts of time planning then laboring toward them with an uncanny perseverance.

"Someone said, 'There are three things that make life worth living: someone to love, something to do, and something to look forward to.' Dreams have to do with the latter. They make life worth living because dreams are what propel life forward. They make tomorrow worth waking up to.

"Anyone can dream a dream. But keeping the dream alive—that is the problem. It's hard to keep a dream alive when, because of the dream, you are freezing to death in a cold, dark prison. It's hard to keep your dream focused when you are run out of town and stoned and left for dead. All of these things and many more happened in the Apostle Paul's life, and yet he never gave up on his dream.

"Given the low expectation level in many of our churches, it is easy to just settle in. Take last year's calendar to the copy machine and run off the calendar for the new year. If you can learn to push the right buttons and keep certain people happy in your church, you can just settle in for the duration. Given these circumstances, it is not easy to keep a great dream alive in your heart. Dreams die easily within the soul. They die when we learn after a few years, that opposition is too strong, and the cost is too high, and the road to our dream is too long and tortuous. One pastor said, 'I feel like a light bulb on the front porch on a summer night. Things keep flying at me in all directions.' A lot of very little things can kill a very large dream if we let them. Where do you turn when you find yourself just settling in?

"A good place I found to begin is the Apostle Paul. When I suddenly realized that I could be an easy victim of this dreadful 'settling in' disease, I thought of the great apostle. He wrote it to the Philippians (3:12) from prison in Rome: 'Brethren, I haven't arrived yet!' or 'I haven't lost my dream here in prison.' Isn't that remarkable? Isn't that inspiring when you realize who it comes from and where it comes from?

"Then I remembered a word from the apostle to young Timothy. You know, young men can also burn out and lose their vision and settle for less than God's best early on in their ministry. Evidently, Paul saw the possibility of young Timothy just settling in and going into survival mode. He challenged him in second Timothy chapter one: 'Stir up the gift of God which is in you.' The language uses the imagery of the glowing embers of a fire that is about to go out. It is a compound word coming from the Greek for a live coal of fire and old-fashioned bellows that were used to rekindle the fire. Clarence Jordan's Cotton Patch Version says: 'Shake the ashes off the God-given fire that is in you.'

"How would he say it if he stood before us today? Maybe with different words but the same meaning, 'Don't let anything destroy your dream. Don't let life's hard and difficult experiences rob you of the dream that God has placed in your heart. Forget what's behind and press forward to what lies before ahead.'"

By 2005, Dad's thoughts on dreaming included anyone on the human journey. "Whatever it is, find something to live for. Find something to do. Find something that will keep you looking up and not looking down—something worth getting up for in the morning."[63]

Putting Christ First Above Loyalty to Family

Dad was acutely aware of the difficulty of interpreting the absurd demands of Jesus in the gospels to North Americans who valued God, family, and country, not necessarily in that order. He also felt the costs of long separations from his family during the Brazil years.

"Our relationship to Christ, if it is all it should be, will be a relationship that takes precedence over all others, even our relationship to our own families. What did the man mean when he said, 'Let me go and bury my father?' He did not mean that his father had already died. If that were the case, he would not have been in the crowd of followers. He means, 'My father is getting old. He could pass away anytime now. I think I should stay around until he passes, then I will follow you.'

"The third man's request seems to be more reasonable: 'Just let me go home and say goodbye to my family members.' Sounds reasonable, doesn't it? But Jesus knows what will happen if he should go home and say goodbye to his parents. Let's suppose this young man went home and said to his family, 'I'm leaving you now. I'm going to follow a man by the name of Jesus. He is a great man who preaches the Gospel, heals the sick, and cares for poor and downtrodden people.' The father says, 'Well, son, where does this man live?' And he would have to say, 'Well, Dad, I don't rightly know. He doesn't seem to have a home. I guess you would say he is a homeless man.' Dad gets a worried wrinkle on his forehead and then he asks, 'Well, what does he do for a living? Does he have a good reputation?' And he would have to say, 'Well, Dad, I don't exactly know what he does for a living. His father was a carpenter, and he learned the trade, but he doesn't seem to have any regular work now. I don't know much about his reputation. Many people are following him and believe in him. But I have heard the authorities are watching him very closely. I've heard some say he could be arrested any day.' Your dad says, 'Now let me see if I get this straight. You are going to leave home, leave us behind, and follow a homeless, unemployed man who is being carefully watched by the authorities who may arrest him at any time? Son, are you out of your mind?' Jesus knows what that young man would face if he were to go back and try to say farewell to his parents; also that branches cannot reach out any farther than the roots have reached out underneath."[64]

The Revelation Looks Upward

Dad was always the cup-is-more-than-half-full kind of a guy in his interpretation of the darkest biblical texts.

"John was permitted in chapter 13 to penetrate into the dark, deep mysteries of evil and its workings upon this earth, but he was not allowed to dwell very long upon it. If you read through the book from beginning to the end, you find that you are not allowed to think for very long about evil's power and influence until suddenly your mind is caught up and your head is lifted up and you begin to look at the heavens and you take the upward look. And that is what has happened here with John. I find that very helpful and refreshing at the beginning of a new year. We need to take that upward look."[65]

Bearing Fruit or Trading Members?

Dr. Glenn Hickey never gave up on the organized church. His last time in church was when I took him to St. Marks in Little Rock in January 2013. A thriving African American congregation of two thousand plus, it was what he aspired the church to be: A light to the world, the living body of Christ, and a joyful place to worship. We stood up, and he sang out like barbershop days. Inside the boundaries of his walker, he moved to the worship, and during the sermon he joined the chorus of loud *Amens!* A senior pastor recognized him from his days as Director of Missions for the Pulaski Association and made a point to visit and express his gratitude after the service.

"Those are the words of Jesus Christ who said in John chapter 15: 'Herein is my father glorified, that you bear much fruit, and so shall you be my disciples.' To be a disciple of Jesus is to bear fruit. And when one does not bear fruit, when a church does not bear fruit, when a Christian life does not bear fruit, Jesus says, its destiny is destruction. It is no longer useful. It is no longer serving the function that God intended. And that is God's curse on everything in his kingdom that does not bear fruit. In just a few Sundays, we will be observing our first anniversary with you, and we have received a good many people into our fellowship. Many people have united with us, as I recall we have fifty new members, and how happy we are to have every one of them. A majority of those came from other Baptist churches, and sometimes we can get our comfort in this, just exchanging members with other churches. You can have this one, I will take that one, so we will exchange and our records will look really good at the end of the year, but that is not the main business we are in. God has called us to bear fruit, to bear fruit in his kingdom, and the curse of God will fall on any church that does not accomplish that divine purpose. May God help us to become the kind of tree, the kind of people who bear fruit in the kingdom of God."[66]

Golf

"Man does not like to admit to his inability or face up to his human weakness. That's the reason I don't play golf anymore. I started playing golf when I was pastor in Wellington, Texas, where they put a golf course around the airport. It was dangerous enough with the airplanes flying over your head, but you get me out on that golf course, and it was really a hazardous place to be. I soon learned that it was the best place in the world for me to make a fool of myself. I gave up golf. I am not interested in golf because it shows my inadequacy. It makes me look bad, and no one wants to be made to look bad, do they?

"That's the problem I think many people have with salvation by grace. We want to do some of it ourselves. We want to participate. We want to somehow contribute our part because it is a part of our human pride to want to save ourselves. Don't think it's strange that Paul goes to such great lengths to argue this point of salvation by grace. Nothing we can do but accept it."[67]

O Repeteco (the Sermon Repeat)

Dad had a deep connection to the natural world and often found transcendent revelation on the beach. *The Star Thrower of Costabel* by Loren Eiseley was retold often so as to manifest it in his life.

"I suppose my favorite place to be in all the world is walking along a tropical beach. For thirteen years, while serving as SBC Missionaries to Brazil, we lived and worked in the seacoast city of Recife. Some of the high moments in my spiritual life have been on the seashore, watching God create a new day at sunrise. Because of my intense love for the seaside, one of my favorite narratives is Loren Eiseley's well-known story of the Star Thrower."

"The sun behind me was pressing upward at the horizon's rim, an ominous red glare amidst the tumbling blackness of the clouds. Ahead of me, over the projecting point, a gigantic rainbow of incredible perfection sprung shimmering into existence. Toward its foot, I discerned a human figure standing, as it seemed to me, within the rainbow. He was gazing at something in the sand. He stooped and flung an object beyond the breaking surf. I labored another half a mile toward him and by the time I reached him, kneeling again, the rainbow had receded ahead of us. In a pool of sand and silt, a starfish thrust its arms up stiffly and was holding its body away from the stifling mud. 'It's still alive,' I ventured. 'Yes,' he said, and with a quick, yet gentle movement, he picked up the star and spun it over my head and far out into the sea. 'It may live if the offshore pull is strong enough,' he said. In a sudden embarrassment for words I said, 'Do you collect shells?' 'Only ones like this,' he said softly, gesturing amidst the wreckage of the shore, 'and only for the living.' He stooped again and skipped another star neatly across the water. 'The stars,' he said, 'throw well. One can help them.'" ("The Star Thrower" from *The Unexpected Universe* by Loren Eiseley)

Dad reflected, "That dimension of existence unknown to the world is the self-giving dimension of the cross. The life giver's cross. The cross that constantly challenges us to love not self but life, the life that God has given us in order that we may give it to others, (to become) the life givers of this world."[68]

In an Hour You Think Not

"I was conducting an exam in a seminary class some years ago in Brazil, and one of my students said 'Professor, I know when the Lord is going to come back.'

"'Oh, you do? That's interesting. Tell me, when the Lord is going to come back?'

"'I know the Lord is going to come back during one of your examinations because the Bible says, 'In an hour that you think not the Lord cometh' and I just never can think during one of your exams.'"[69]

The Holy Spirit as Wind

"Many times, I had casually watched the young boys flying their handmade kites in the coastal winds of Recife, where we served fourteen years as Southern Baptist missionaries. But this time it was different. I stopped to observe. These were kids from the dirtiest slums, and their ragged clothes hung loosely on their bodies. Some were probably street kids without a home. They may have seen days without a decent meal. But from sticks and scraps of paper collected from some trash heap, they had they had constructed their crudely built little kites. From somewhere they had scrounged a ball of string. I shot several minutes of videotape just following the course of their kites in the wind. I taped their happy, excited, and sometimes disappointed faces as they saw their tiny kites sail high into the sky or become tangled in a power wire above or come crashing disastrously to the ground. From the very simplest things, cast aside as worthless, they had made an experience of joy and excitement. (*Transformational Journeys* Journal, 2000)

What made the difference? The difference was in the wind. The kites were moved by *Ruach*, (Hebrew word for wind or breath) the Holy Spirit wind that hovers between the seen and the unseen. It was the wind that took those worthless sticks and scraps of paper and made them into a thing of joy to behold. The excitement came when they lifted their fragile creations and gave them up to the wind.

"We often forget the truth because we assume the power is within ourselves: Our knowledge, our human resources, our human ingenuity. We build great buildings and raise massive budgets. We hire the brightest and the best to staff the church. We employ the best consultants and the latest techniques. We think by doing so we can match the power of the world. Not so! God said it through Zechariah long ago, and it is just as true today: 'Not by might, not by power, (that is, human power) but by the spirit saith the Lord of Hosts.' (Zac 5:6)

"God communicates that warmth of the spirit fire through spirit-filled Christians whose lives just seem to radiate that spirit warmth to others. In a world that is often so cold and cruel, so filled with alienation and loneliness, churches of the Lord Jesus Christ need to radiate that warmth and acceptance. No church can in its own power create that…. Only the presence of the Spirit of God can give to worship that feeling of spiritual warmth, that sense of the surrounding presence of the Lord."

"Life in the spirit, dear people of God, will not always be predictable. There will always be an element of mystery and surprise. That is precisely what Jesus was saying to Nicodemus. His was the world of the Pharisee: well ordered; precise rules of conduct; sacred, long-kept traditions. Jesus was saying, 'Nicodemus, you may not be ready to step into this new world, where life is no longer under your control.'

"If you must have a church life or a personal life that is ordered and predictable and without surprises, you are unprepared for life in the

Spirit. If you wish to come to church every Sunday and find things always the same, you are not ready for Spirit-led church. But if you don't mind being totally surprised by God, you are ready. If you want to see things happen in your life or your church that you thought would never happen, you are ready. And most of all, if you are willing to relinquish control, you are ready! Set your sails to catch the wind of the spirit!"[70]

THE RICH BLESSING OF HAVING FRIENDS

I remember that retirement for my parents in Benton, Arkansas was a season of thirst in an unexpected friendship desert. They thrived on the intermittent visits of retired missionaries but were challenged in local friending. They were elated when retired Brazil missionaries James and Betty Wilson (James and Betty Wilson, I.M.B. Missionaries, Equatorial Brazil, 1964–1972) moved in down the street and enjoyed Brazilian born MK Bob Berry and his wife, Diane Berry, (son of Brazil Missionaries Ed and Lois Berry; brother to MKs Laura Spiegel and Daniel Berry) as one of their ministers.

"Now this man had four friends. He was richly blessed with friends. He could not walk and had to have someone take him everywhere he went. There were no motorized wheelchairs in those days. They had heard of Jesus and his ministry of healing, how he could give sight to the blind, and enable the lame to walk…. When his friends heard Jesus was nearby in his home in Capernaum, they said, 'We can carry you to Jesus'…. What they didn't realize that many others had the same idea, so when they approached the house there was already a great crowd gathered in and around the house. But these were friends. They were determined friends. They were committed friends. They were friends who did not give up easily. Now the house Jesus lived in was like most of the houses in Palestine in that day. They were adobe construction, made of clay and straw, sometimes crude bricks, with a flat roof and steps going up one side of the house to the adobe roof. These friends looked the situation over and decided the only way to get their paralyzed friend to Jesus was to carry him up those steps to the top of the house, dig a hole in the adobe roof and let him down into the room where Jesus was. And that is exactly what they did. Without those four friends by his side, this man would never have been healed. We all need friends like that, don't we?"

"When we retired in 1995, we moved to Benton and built a new home in the country. We began to attending Benton First Baptist Church. They were a friendly church, nothing negative to say about the fine people in that church, but we soon learned how hard it is to establish close friendships with other people in a large church. Someone must take the initiative in starting a friendship and I might as well be that one."

"We are all like the paralytic at some time in life. We will always face times when we need help, times in life when we cannot face the battles of life all alone. Having friends in a time of great need may make all the difference."

"A story is told of Jackie Robinson, the first African American to play major league baseball. While breaking baseball's color barrier, he faced jeering crowds in every stadium. Playing one day in his home stadium in Brooklyn, he committed an error. His own fans began to ridicule him. He stood at second base, humiliated, while the fans jeered. Then his friend shortstop "PeeWee" Reese came over and stood next to him. He put his arm around Jackie Robinson and faced the crowd. The fans grew quiet. Robinson later said that arm around his shoulder saved his career."[71]

Glenn the Dad

In the late 1980s, the age of family therapy as social norm was in full force and vogue both in Kansas City, MO and Broadway Baptist Church, where I was a member. The intensity of worship that some therapists in my circles enjoyed was annoying. My friend and Spiritual Director at that time, David Young, eventually persuaded me that a father/son clearing of the air would be good for both of us if Dad would agree to it.

The idea of resolving the unfinished work with parents was the *onda do dia* (fashion of the day) and crystalized my own unexpressed anger toward my father that had simmered for years. In my view, he was usually out of the house ministering, being a pastor, a teacher, a hero, but often an absent father. Mom was always present, but to be with my dad, we needed a bicycle or road trip, which while loads of fun, came rarely. So, I set up a meeting with my dad with a therapist of my choice. He appeared surprisingly eager to meet with someone who by the nature of the beast was already my ally, knowing my side of the story, and invested in my psycho-welfare.

Michael Reeser was as skilled as they come in family reconciliation interventions. He began by asking Dad to explain his relationship with his father, Glenn Hickey.

Michael: "How much time did you get to spend with your dad?"

Glenn: "Twice a year he actually sat down and played with us, our birthdays and Christmas. All other days he was driven, all business and chores."

Michael: "So would it be fair to say you did not learn to play with your father?"

Glenn: Resounding laughter, then "Yes, he only gave us what his father gave to him." He appeared keenly aware of what was coming next.

Michael: "Well, Daniel has asked for this meeting because he wanted to express some things."

Glenn: "I understand"

So, then I poured my heart out, basically summarizing the years feeling undervalued and second choice to my dad's ministry career.

There was a long silence, then we noticed tears from my father. They were beautiful and vulnerable.

Glenn: "Well, then, I know what you say is true, what can I do now?"

I then asked for my dad's blessing on my life, which I suspected was available but never fully expressed.

It suddenly became the most significant moment I ever had with my father. He laid hands on my head and prayed beautifully, and I felt power coming out of him and into myself in a way that has always filled the rest of my life with liberation and joy. We both cried and were profoundly united from that moment on.

Forgiveness

The reconciling father/son therapy event of 1985 put Dad and me on the same page. All was forgiven and experienced through the prism of that event thereafter.

After her famous frankness in the moment, my mother would apologize if in her judgement she hurt someone, including me. We were close during my adolescent years, and it pained me if I embarrassed her. When I was thirteen, I conspired with my ingenious MK neighbor Ray Fleet, Jr. (MK son of Ray and Ruby Fleet, I.M.B. Missionaries, North Brazil, 1964–1994) and we blew up a guava tree with powder from about 50 firecrackers stuffed into a pipe. The explosion and destruction were far greater than we anticipated, causing embarrassment for my mom with the neighbors. I profusely apologized, and she forgave me with the same enthusiasm that she had expressed her disgust.

"Lynda Taylor was killed by a truck driver who had been behind the wheel for twenty hours straight. A tractor trailer rig driven by Billy Turnbow plowed into Lynda Taylor's car near a construction zone. The family had every reason to seek the maximum penalty when the driver pleaded guilty to manslaughter. Lynda was eight months pregnant. Her twin three-year-old daughters were injured but recovered. Instead of pushing for a harsh sentence, the Taylor family urged the judge to be lenient on the driver, who has a wife and two young children.

"Bryan Hancock, the brother of Lynda Taylor, said: 'Lynda's children have lost their mother, and we couldn't find a constructive reason for the Turnbow children to lose their father. Turnbow had no intention to harm anyone. We thank him for his apology.' Harold Hancock, Lynda Taylor's father, is a Baptist pastor. He said: 'We are a family whose faith is important to us. We have a deep and abiding faith in our Lord and our Christ. We had to forgive Mr. Turnbow, just as Christ has forgiven us.'

"Many people think they believe in the concept of forgiveness, or at least they say they do when they study it in Sunday school. But Lynda Taylor's family clearly lives it. If the Taylors can forgive their huge loss, surely, we should be quick to forgive lesser harms. Forgiveness is costly business."[72]

Irish Blessings

Dad fulfilled another travel dream of an Irish Spring in 1996 when he took us to cycle the Emerald Isle. Cycling offers mystical moments when the purr of the spinning spokes and rising wind in the ears on downhill rides at near 60 mph gels into body/machine mindfulness, following the perfect fall line down the green and rocky slopes. In Ireland this could only be spoiled abruptly by the endless sheep crossings on the road.

Early on the trip a bit of magic happened that set the key of high notes for the next two weeks. Hickeys have Irish roots, and we were all about chatting it up with our kin, if we could find any. We had planned to *roust-about* Galway in County Claire, but a serendipitous encounter with two Catholic priests set us on another path.

"You lads should really go to the *Connemara*. It's just splendid up there."

"Okay, you talked us into it." Dad was never shy about a change of plans, especially if a new adventure was offered. We set off the next April morning in the paradoxical embrace of warm sunshine and cool breeze of the mountains ascending to the townland of *Glassilaun*.

An unexpected pub came up exactly when we were ready for a respite, lonely and magical complete with live music for as long as we pleased to listen. We were the only visitors, and apparently rare in this hour, and they played with a fervor unmatched. They anointed us with mournful songs of their homeland, Northern Ireland.

The blessing of the pub in Glassilaun, County Claire, Ireland.

Refugees from Protestant-Catholic violence, they played themselves some healing balm. Sensing my dad's tears and delirium, I was not about to leave. "How can I express my gratitude," he asked me softly, as if I were an expert in pub culture.

"I think, Dad, you offer to buy them a round."

"Yes!"

He waited for the next pause and declared in his best Irish Arkansas brogue, "I want to by a round for all. This music has blessed me so much!" There were smiling nods, a round was promptly served, and the music quickly picked up again with more intensity.

And so it was that a previously tee-totaling Southern Baptist preacher bought a round of Guinness for a bar full of North and South, Protestant and Catholic Irishmen.

The eastern coast of Ireland's Britta's Bay is forever beach that is overwhelming in its simple curl of sands as you come out of the high grasses. We were in the goodbye chapter of the trip to this beloved and mystical country. Dad walked ahead. I had lingered to take in the panoramic view imagining the English coast and beyond. The trip had been a healing door to my reconstruction from a second divorce. I was catching up to him on the forever beach and noticed his gasping. I thought it was an allergy or semi emergency. No, he was weeping, and what a funny place to do it! "Dad...are you okay? What's going on?"

"Oh, just reflecting on my life with such gratitude, it's been..." And his speech trailed off into more emotion.

It was a definite leave-Dad-alone moment, so we walked quite separately for what could have been miles, in a close but distant tunnel of father/son reunion. It was only years later, shortly after he passed, that I interpreted at least part of those Britta's Bay tears were for my second marriage, which had just ended.

The Wounded Healer

In his view, Dad's neuropathy in his last years enabled him to become a wounded healer and reach out to more folks with visible and invisible wounds. He was fragile on his walker but enjoyed surprising audiences with his keen mind and spirit. Such a day was had at Calvary Baptist Church in Little Rock, when Dr. Ed Simpson, (Dr. Clyde Glazener, Dad's friend and pastor during the Baptist conflict years, had migrated to Fort Worth, Texas, to become pastor of Gambrell Street Baptist Church) Dad's Pastor, hosted "Glenn Hickey Day" to celebrated Dad's 60 years of ministry. "The people laughed, and so enjoyed his words, and the message was biblical, applicable, and impactful." (Dr. Ed Simpson, Interview, 2016)

Henri Nouwen's book *The Wounded Healer*, about ministering to hurting and severely disabled people in the communal setting of a Catholic community was a fountain for Dad's winter years. "There are all kinds of healers in our health-conscious world, and the reason for all this is that we are all imperfect, wounded creatures living in a wounded, disjointed, and sinful world. Physically, emotionally, mentally, or spiritually, we are wounded people. The big question is not how we can hide our wounds, or how can we compensate for our wounds or put them on display, but how can we put our woundedness into service for others. How can we employ them for a redemptive purpose?

"Woundedness is nothing to be ashamed of. Ignore those glances of disdain or pity that the thoughtless may cast at you. You are God's child, created in his image regardless of what others may say or think. Wear your woundedness proudly. *I want to say it again, wear your woundedness proudly.* Use your woundedness to heal others of theirs. In your woundedness there is strength. In your woundedness there is power and authentication. In your woundedness you can speak more clearly, you can be heard when you speak."[73]

Traffic

He was temperate in speech, except when in later years Humvees started appearing on the roads, which offended him to the core. He did not think they belonged in civilian traffic and were driven by showoffs. Once one cut him off in Little Rock, and he let them have it with a loud proclamation: "What a jackass!"

The News Cycle Interpreter

Dad was always eager to follow the current events in his community and the world. Before the internet, he subscribed to *National Geographic* and always tried to find what was available in international print. He would relish a copy of the *New York Times* brought in by someone at the airport in Recife, Brazil. When in the United States, he often relied on the CBS evening news with Walter Cronkite and later admired Dan Rather. His *café com leite* was a brew of secular news and sacred texts, consumed daily. He gained inspiration from the good news stories of unlikely heroes and Don Quixote-like conquests, looking for the sacred hidden in the secular and profane.

Really how different is the year 2020 from the year 1980 in the human experience of the world as moving too fast? Alvin Toffler's *Future Shock*,[74] was a confirmation of Dad's experience of human resistance to change regardless of geography and culture. He had just left Recife, Brazil, and Batesville, Arkansas was not so very different.

"Alvin Toffler has talked about the kind of world we live in as fast-moving in his book *Future Shock* and has described that the rapid tech changes and transformation of our society are more than many people can cope. It reminds me of when I was a child. I used to go every year to the county fair in Montgomery County, Arkansas, and the thing I liked most was the merry-go-round. Not just to ride it, but I would stand there and watch it for hours on end, if Mother and Dad would let me. I liked to get up just as close as I could to the merry-go-round, with the horses whirling by, as they go up and down as they passed by. I stood so close that they formed just a blur before my eyes. Sometimes our world becomes like that, a blur before our eyes because things are happening that change our lives, and they're upsetting, and disturbing, and perplexing, and we cannot understand the meaning of it all."[75]

The Liberation of the Fifty-Two Hostages

The daily frustration of no resolution of the four-hundred, forty-four-day Iran-Hostage crisis was wearing on my parents, as they felt personally the pain of their President and the country.

"There are some things in life that become indelibly stamped upon our mind so that we can never forget them. They become a permanent part of our life and the visual images that make up our past. The assassination of President Kennedy was such an event. I believe that the liberation of the fifty-two American hostages from captivity will never go away, or at least it has had that sort of impact on my life because there is something in that event symbolic for us, for freedom-loving Americans. Who did not feel a lump in his throat or wipe a tear from his eye as he saw that scene of joy and triumph as those fifty-two hostages stepped off the plane in Wiesbaden, Germany? The word 'freedom' will never be the same because it has been redefined as the fruit of patience. The word 'patience' has been used for the long and complicated process, involving many countries and many different people, that our former President Jimmy Carter has exercised to accomplish this great victory."[76]

Space Shuttle Return

Dad rarely missed a N.A.S.A. space launch, it was food for his nerdy soul.

"I watched the return of the space shuttle last Tuesday, and I was fascinated by that. There is something about these things that grab me. When you think about all the intricacy of a mission like that: The human resources, the technical know-how, the different things that must move and work together in perfect timing, and so many thousands of people scattered around this earth, technicians, tracking stations, electronic wizards, and engineers all functioned in sync. I watched as they brought that space shuttle back, and as we looked in on Mission Control in Houston, Texas, and they celebrated the return of that space shuttle, a perfect flight. 'I said to myself, oh, if only the church of Jesus Christ could somehow get it together, every person in their place, everything timed and planned, and worked out and timed to precision, everyone doing his job.' I sensed that as I looked onto a kind of unity, a kind of singlemindedness that was a beautiful thing. Why can't we model that in the greatest mission on the face of this earth, the mission of reaching people for Jesus Christ?"[77]

Hiroshima or World Hunger?

President Harry Truman was originally raised a Baptist, and at the age of 18, was baptized at the Benton Boulevard Baptist Church in Kansas City. "Later, as a young man, Truman described himself in a letter to his sweetheart, Bess Wallace, as a 'Lightfoot Baptist.' He told her that the Baptists 'do not want a person to go to shows or dance or do anything for a good time. Well I like to do all those things and play cards besides. So, you see I'm not very strong as a Baptist. Anyhow I don't think any church on earth will take you to heaven if you're not real anyway. I believe in people living what they believe and talking afterwards."

Mom was 15 and Dad was 14 on August 6th, 1945, when the bomb dropped on Hiroshima, and that event was seared into their beings. They loved reminiscing about the straight-talking Baptist President Harry Truman, but could not avoid the deep ambivalence about what their country did to end the war.

"Did you notice the other day, the commemoration? We saw it on television, the bombing of Hiroshima, Japan, where one hundred thousand people died in an instant, the dropping of an atomic bomb. Thirty-five years after that happened, we are still remembering it. Someone has said that every three or four days, that many children die around our world of hunger because of malnutrition and the health complications that it brings. We never get too worried or upset about it because no one has set off a bomb. It happens silently, and yet it's going on day after day.

"I have a friend who is very concerned about this and he says this: 'I cannot do everything, but I can do something, and what I can do, I must do.' He is not a wealthy man at all. He is a seminary professor, and his family does without meat one day a week, and they take the money they save and give it to world hunger. He walks every day to his classes at the seminary, calculates how much that saves, and gives that to world hunger. Such little things, and yet that's what Jesus is talking about in this parable. You can give a cup of cold water to a stranger in the name of Jesus. You can find a stranger who has moved into your neighborhood who needs to know friendship, are you doing that, in the name of Jesus?"[78]

Entering the Third Millennium

"There is much that is new in the world of the twenty-first century. Modern technology has made the world into a much different world than the one I grew up in on a thirty-five-acre farm in Montgomery

County, Arkansas. But the spiritual realities of our Third Millennium world are basically unchanged. Millions of people are still lost and in need of forgiveness. Many still struggle with loneliness, hunger, starvation, and the ravages of war and natural disasters. An estimated forty thousand people have died in Venezuela from devastating floods. Our world is an aching, hurting, and needy world. The twenty-first century is perhaps the most challenging and exciting opportunity for the Gospel of Jesus Christ since the first century."[79]

The Survivalist Movement

"I submit to you today that our posture as Christians in the world in which you and I live is not to be one of survival, but rather one of revival because God has called us to be agents of redemption, to be witnesses to the glorious gospel of Jesus Christ, to be those who have within them the life, the everlasting life, the overflowing abundant life of Jesus Christ, and we should be sharing it with others in preparation for that great and glorious day of the Lord and his judgment upon all mankind."[80]

The Iraq War

"We are now engaged in an ugly war in Iraq that seems to have no end. What is the answer? What is the solution? Only in the spirit of God can men and women who fight and destroy one another ever be made to come together and sit down at the table of peace. The Bible teaches us to pray for peace. The Bible says, 'Pray for the peace of Jerusalem. We ought to pray for the peace of Jerusalem and peace in all the Arab world.' In the spirit of God, we can pray that prayer for peace, even among those who are our enemies."[81]

Jimmy Carter and Something More Important

"Joy continues with a confidence that God is with us for the long haul and will never give up on us. Look at Philippians 1:6 (N.I.V.) where Paul says: 'Being confident of this, that he who began a good work in you will carry it on to completion until the day of Christ Jesus.' Just remember, whatever may come your way, however severe may be the trial in life, God is not through with you yet.

"When President Jimmy Carter was defeated by Ronald Reagan in the 1980 election, it came as a devastating blow. He felt he had so much more to do for the service of his country. There is an interesting story in connection with that defeat. Robert Drinan is a Catholic priest, now a professor at Georgetown University, but for ten years he was a member of the U.S. Congress. In the final days of the Carter administration, Drinan learned that, due to a change in canon law, he would have to give up his seat in congress to remain in the priesthood.

"He attended the annual Christmas party for Congress at the White House. Both he and Carter found it difficult to be in a festive mood. They were both depressed. Drinan wanted to continue in the legislature, and Carter was very disappointed that he could not continue another term as president. When Father Drinan approached President Carter in the reception line, Carter flashed that typical Carter grin and said, 'Father, God must have something more important for us to do.'

"And indeed, he did… So today, Jimmy Carter now builds houses for the poor. He builds bridges of peace between people who are fighting each other. He tackles some of the most devastating diseases though the Carter Center and teaches Sunday school class in his hometown church of Plains, Georgia. Father Drinan now finds his ministry multiplied as he teaches students at Georgetown University. That is why Paul says in verse 12: 'Now I want you to know, brothers and sisters, that what has happened to me has actually served to advance the gospel.' If you would find joy in all circumstances of life, hold fast to the confidence that God has started something in you and will keep on working His good in you until the very end.'"[82]

After the Brazil years, Dad was less attached to a country and more drawn to the invisible Kingdom of God. This sermon was first preached at Memorial Baptist Church in Little Rock on the eve of Independence Day 2003 and then four more times in Little Rock churches, always on the eve of the Fourth of July.

"I am happy to be a citizen of the United States of America, aren't you? I am even happier to be a Christian, aren't you? A proud citizen of the Kingdom of heaven! You know, I didn't know just how happy I was to be a citizen of this country until I left it for fourteen years. I didn't know how happy I would be to see the Statue of Liberty in New York Harbor, until I saw it returning from living overseas.

"In this single verse in Galatians, the Apostle Paul reminds us of some very important truths that we need to re-examine and reaffirm as we approach the day we celebrate our American freedom. 'Stand fast therefore in the liberty by which Christ has made us free, and do not be entangled again with a yoke of bondage' (Gal. 5:1) ....So don't ever let anyone force you to affirm something or do something that goes against your Christian conscience. Jesus died on the cross to set us free, not to enslave us with someone's idea or doctrine or way of life....Let me just say in closing that the greatest of all freedoms is the spiritual freedom we have in Christ.

"Freedom's pinnacle was not reached at Philadelphia in the signing of the Declaration of Independence, not in the bloody battles of Lexington and Concord, not even long ago at the Red Sea when God delivered his people from Egyptian bondage. Freedom's pinnacle, freedom's crowning glory, came when a man who was both God and man walked up Calvary's hill with a cross and died upon that cross to set us forever free from the shackles of sin and slavery! Thank God I am an American (Citizen of the U.S.A.), but thank God most of all that I am a Christian, a born-again child of God!"[83]

Reverend Don Cooper remembers the first sermon Dad delivered after the tragedy of 9-11. "He had some wonderful sermons. I remember the sermon Sunday night after 9-11. I was interim pastor at

Crossroads Baptist church out in Saline County. I had him out, and I remember the title of the sermon 'What to Do with Your Fears.' One of the illustrations was that the morning of 9-11, as he referenced it, he was at the breakfast table. He and Dorothy were there together, and as he watched it, he said: 'America, welcome to the real world.'"

"A Brazilian national said to us one day, to a group of North American missionaries, 'Don't bring us your American way of life. Bring us Jesus, yes, but the American way of life we do not need here. We can't afford it. We do not have the material base to provide it for our people, so don't talk to us about the American way, talk to us about Jesus.'"[84]

Dad admired the triple citizenship of the Apostle Paul, who identified as Jewish, Roman, and a citizen of the Kingdom of God. Brazil transformed his identity into a Global Christian, and he leaned into Paul's declaration in Galatians 3:28, "There is neither Jew nor Gentile, neither slave nor free, nor is there male and female, for you are all one in Christ Jesus." (N.I.V.)

Missionary Steve reflects on Missionary Glenn

"In the early 1970s, the Hickey family, Glenn, Dorothy, and Danny, arrived from Brazil to stay during their time of furlough. Danny and I were the same age, so we had time to get to know one another through the youth program of our church. We became good friends during that year. I remember that Uncle Glenn always seemed more 'real' and less interested than most missionaries in only talking about his work and ministry. He would usually tell family stories that connected with me in a way that made me want to go to Brazil someday. After that year, they left and did not return to our church again for many years.

"I was surprised, after transferring to Ouachita Baptist University, to find that Dan Hickey was in his freshman year there, too. Living in the same dorm and playing on the soccer team together made it easy to rekindle the friendship we'd formed in high school. Reconnecting with Dan, meeting and becoming friends with many of his MK (missionary kids) friends, gave me an even broader understanding of missions from their perspective. My growing friendship with Dan led to him asking me to spend the summer with his family in Brazil. After checking with my parents, and assuming Dan had checked with his, (he hadn't) the plan was made. After school was out that semester, we headed to Recife, Brazil where I'd spend the next few months with the Hickey family.

"After recovering graciously from my surprise arrival, I believe Uncle Glenn and Aunt Dorothy were excited to show me the place they loved and had adopted as their new home. They all wanted me to participate in as much as possible. Looking back, I see that God used these normal daily activities and meeting needs in the lives of others to speak to my own heart about the possibility of mission work someday.

"I was treated as a MK the rest of the summer by the whole mission family. I got to see and often sample many of the wonderful things that make Brazil great. The food, the soft drink *Guaraná*, soccer, singing, worship styles, the welcoming way of the Brazilian people, and, of course, the beautiful beaches, where we spent a lot of our time. We camped. We took bike trips to different parts of Northeast Brazil and traveled from Recife to Salvador for the annual mission meeting. There were so many different ways to learn about this beautiful country and its people. Uncle Glenn was a key part of allowing me to put myself into it fully.

"And speaking of the beaches, as normal nineteen-year-old young men, we especially noticed the unique swimsuits worn by the ladies, known as *tangas*. (I later learned this word was Portuguese for 'thongs!') The fact that the suits left little to the imagination did not bother me in the least and I took it all in stride!

"Many years later, after answering God's call in our own lives to international missions, Kathy and I were appointed as new missionaries to Southern Africa. Following our appointment service, Uncle Glenn came up to me, looked me in the eye, and said, 'Steve, I believe during the summer you spent with us in Brazil, you saw a lot more than those *tangas*!' I laughed with him and replied, 'Yes sir, I believe I did.'

"If I took the time to sit and reflect on people who have been 'difference makers' in my life, Glenn Hickey, or Uncle Glenn as I knew him, would be near the top of that list."
(Stephen and Kathy Dewbre were IMB Missionaries to Southern Africa, 1989-2009; and IMB Member Care Missionaries to the Americas, 2010-2015)

Rent

"Five hundred twenty-five thousand six hundred minutes, Five hundred twenty-five thousand moments so dear." ("Seasons of Love" by Jonathan Larson, from *Rent*, the Broadway Musical)

Our nuclear family of Hickeys were shameless criers. Mom and Dad cried at my American School of Recife Master of Ceremony presentations for talent show night, and that was supposed to be comedy! On an evening in March 2010, Dad and I were lachrymose at the men's chorus rendition of *Rent* at Trinity United Methodist Church in Little Rock. The evening had already been emotional, since the guest pianist/conductor was the renowned Mark Hayes, a dear friend of ours from Kansas City and a *Transformational Journeys* veteran of the millennium 2000 Brazil adventure with Dad. Before presenting a Brazilian Bossa Nova-inspired medley, he made a point of asking Dad to stand, introducing his legacy to the full house and enthusiastic applause. We were quite misty-eyed.

The men's chorus later rendered a stirring version of "Seasons" that was the balm we needed. Mom was not doing well, and we were beginning to measure our seasons with her.

The Caretaker

Dad's love for Mom, in my experience, was a cross between the honey darlin' Arkansas mushy mush and a hard-won respect born of living together overseas as partners for many years. Music was the eternal connection, displayed most vulnerably and nobly in their gospel duets. Audiences in north and south were inspired by their harmony and *Alegria* in English and Portuguese.

Mom and Dad joined Parkway Village Retirement Community ahead of their time in 2005. It was a surprise to friends and family that Dad was already "seeing thru the glass darkly" (I Cor. 13:12) and knew something was amiss. A "probable Alzheimer's dementia" diagnosis for Mom came only four years later.

In the first year after this confirmation, Dad rose every morning early and prayed for an hour. His prayers were as ardent, human, and faithful as their fifty-plus years of partnership marriage. He surely wanted an easier path but accepted each stage of the damnable disease with the courage to fight what could be fought for Mom and the agile grace to receive and celebrate the remaining moments of presence.

One of the sweet, sweet answers to his prayers was that Mom did not lose her gift of piano that had blessed so many. This was Dad's miracle, that her brilliant musical mind even into the thick wilderness of a disease had retained the old piano-pounding mastery of the *Corinhos* (Portuguese hymns) and English Stamps-Baxter Quartet melodies. She continued to enchant friends with the "Dorothy Magic," and Dad wept for joy often.

"Dorothy played the old songs with joy at mission meeting programs in Brazil. We all enjoyed singing,
'*Mairzy doats and dozy doats and liddle lamzy divey*
'*A kiddley divey too, wouldn't you?*
'*These words sound queer, and funny to your ear, a little jumbled and jivy,*
'*Mares eat oats and does eat oats and little lambs eat ivy.*
'*A kid will eat ivy too, wouldn't you?*'"

"In later years, we went to visit Dorothy and Glenn at Parkway Village, and her memory loss was already getting pretty bad. You couldn't have a conversation with her, but Glenn said 'Dorothy, why don't you play for us?' She played and remembered every song, and I was touched that God had allowed her to remember those promises, the music was still there. Glenn confined himself to care for her, and we observed that she was nicely dressed, her hair neatly combed, and I know she couldn't do that herself. Glenn baked cookies and went about giving them away to homebound neighbors, so that way he received contact with other people." (Source: Glenda and Dave Miller Interview, 2016)

Dad for his part coped by reaching out to friends and family, and preaching when he was invited. In the last year, he moved Mom to the Mount Ida nursing home where more than eighty percent of patients were cared for by professionals who knew them before they became patients. It also put us closer to an incredible resource, Aunt Glenna and Uncle Bob Lybrand. They became the divine manifestation of steadfastness and strength as we grew weak from the final onslaught of the persistent losses that Alzheimer's inflicts on the family who remembers the incredible gift and love that is now vanishing. Hot meals, a steady caring presence, and even apartment cleaning and organization were always offered with sensitivity and wisdom. When Mom passed into the light in May of 2010, it was Aunt Glenna who showed up first as the holy presence to begin the testimonies of a life well lived.

I was less than a model caretaker for Mom during the later stages of her Alzheimer's. I would be present in the room but was unable to completely engage as a son when she was no longer herself or confused me with my dad. A compassionate nurse noticed and tried to instruct me in how to care for her in her present state of being. "Get up in her face and talk to her!" She would then model it so well, like Mom was her own dear mother. I mustered the courage to try it a few times but never adapted into this new way of being. If we are fortunate to live long enough, life invites us to love our parents like they once loved us. I missed opportunities with my mom at the end, and trust I was forgiven. The *Espirito Santo* in her was present and still reaching out.

Dad and Mom's Brazil missionary colleagues chose to err on the side of discretion when it came to discussing temporal powers. (A helpful synonym for the word politics that stresses the temporary nature of political power in any age. Great powers rise and fall. Elected leaders in democracies are temporary. This contrasts with sacred or eternal power, which transcends the temporal.)[85] They were strictly admonished by the I.M.B. not to bring up temporal powers or the Brazilian military dictatorship anytime, anywhere. Dad was particularly careful, judging it prudent to avoid public opinions on politicians or hotly debated issues for most of his career. I never exercised this same caution, expressing my passion for George McGovern and his promise to end the Vietnam War to the shock of my Nixon-supporting Grandfather Glenn in 1972.

In their expatriate consciousness, my parents' calling was about eternal matters deep into the human heart and soul, and this held their attention. The Brazilian Military Coup of 1964 was evident by occasional tanks in the streets or rumors of violence, but stayed largely in the subconscious. It was at first easy to keep American current events out of sight. This strategy failed as the assassination of JFK in 1964, the men on the moon in 1969, and the Vietnam War became topics across Brazil and in the strong opinions expressed by students at the seminary in Recife.

A window into Dad's synthesis of temporal power and his practice of Christianity was opened when we started our 1975 European cycling tour by attending the Rock Opera "Jesus Christ Superstar" in London. At the time protested virulently by Jews and Christians, He was wide-eyed to accusations of profaning the sacred in presenting a Rock Passionate drama. I have always been grateful to him for having the courage to introduce this and trust my response. When the disciples sing the catchy "What's the Buzz, tell me what's happening?" the explosive and soul-piercing Jesus tenor response follows, "Why should you want to know, don't you mind about the future, don't you try to think ahead? Save tomorrow for tomorrow, think about today instead." This Jesus gave me eternal goosebumps and a fountain of hope for my Christian sojourn ahead. With Dad, the Holy was already waiting for us in the world; his was a humble curiosity to find and affirm the sacred in such temporal places as political parties, foreign policy, and rock musicals.

We only began to enjoy discussing these matters after the crucible of Brazil, when I was a Master of Divinity student between 1980 and 1983 at Midwestern Baptist Theological Seminary in Kansas City. Our "one more coffee after breakfast" talks always started with current events and usually ended with our synthesis of what people of faith and temporal powers should be doing about the great issues of the day. We were short on solutions, but became proficient at deepening our questions. We usually chose harmony over the unspoken potential for disagreements. Through the influence of German theologian Reinhold Niebuhr, he had clarity on the relationship between the eternal and temporal powers. "For Niebuhr, theology and temporal power are not really separate fields, but two perspectives on a single reality, each helping to illumine the data of the other. His central concerns clearly bridge the two disciplines: the nature and destiny of man, the perplexities of social ethics, and the conditions of human community."[86]

Dad observed the striking parallels between the increasing national division in the temporal powers as expressed in movements within the Democratic and Republican parties, and the Southern Baptist schism of 1979. His key metric to evaluate world leaders was their capacity for statesmanship or how skilled they became at crafting the peace and the common good above tribal, partisan, and national interests.

His nexus of inspiration for living out the gospel had begun to shift from Billy Graham to Martin Luther King Jr. This is not a radical leap of faith, since Graham's early crusades carried a prophetic message with echoes of M.L.K. that exposed the darker side of patriotism.

Known as one of the foremost world authorities on the gnostic gospels, Dr. Elaine Pagels had a "born again" experience at a 1958 Billy Graham Crusade in San Francisco when she was fifteen. The young preacher at first astonished her with his clear condemnation of America for dropping the atom bombs on Hiroshima and Nagasaki that killed over one hundred thousand civilians. When Graham gave no comfort to "Christians who used scripture to justify slavery and defend racism while ignoring the poor and our own spiritual poverty," in her words, "I was riveted."[87]

Jimmy Carter was held in deepest esteem for his 1978 Camp David Accords, which brought lasting peace between Israel and Egypt, confirmed in 2002 when he won the Nobel Peace Prize. They had seen firsthand the Carters' work reach all the way to Recife, Brazil through the Pernambuco/Georgia Partners of the Americas. I stood in line for an hour in Kansas City to get President Carter's signature on his 2005 book, "Our Endangered Values." The look on Dad's face later was worth the wait.

Dad accepted my invitation to go one evening to the Obama 2008 campaign headquarters in Little Rock to make phone calls. It was always a mixture of white and black folks dominated by African American grandmothers, who were always there in big numbers and in my mind had a large say in putting Barack into the White House. This evening we were making our calls using the state-of-the-art call lists, suggested opening scripts, and responses. The goal was to determine the preference of the voter, and ask for them to volunteer if they said Obama. I called a few with the expected strong responses both negative and positive. I asked Dad if he wanted to make a call, and to my astonishment he said an enthusiastic yes! He ignored the script as soon as he realized he had dialed a close buddy who just happened to be on our list. He was laughing out loud immediately, reveled in the serendipity, and never did tell me which way his friend was voting.

I was not surprised that he voted for Obama, since he was impressed that Reinhold Niebuhr was the candidate's theologian of choice. He despised the consequences of the Iraq War, and after careful study concluded that the Affordable Care Act would lift many people up. (He was incensed with the "donut hole" in his own Medicare coverage, when he was forced to pay thousands of dollars for meds every year). It felt like being on the cusp of something new to stand in a long line at the Thompson Library in Little Rock to vote together for this Audacity of Hope. Obama continued to inspire Dad in the nuclear peacemaking initiative to Iran in April of 2009, followed quickly by reaching out to Cuba with intense diplomacy. We were shocked that he won the Nobel Peace Prize that same year, believing that it was too soon in his presidency.

After voting again for Obama in 2012, for the first time in his life that I am aware he shared this choice with select friends and family. There was shock and awe from Christians close to him, and he reciprocated with deep respect for their opinions. He remained proud of his unprecedented President and astonishingly detached from the temporal power of politics. In other words, he never saw the point in posting a political opinion on Facebook.

Reinhold Niebuhr's Serenity Prayer was a mantra in his elder years, "God grant me the serenity to accept the things I cannot change, courage to change the things I can, and wisdom to know the difference."

Money

My Grandpa Glenn Hickey was a skilled businessman and amassed a fortune in the Mount Ida hardware enterprise, but raised Glenn and Glenna insisting on frugality and hard work. Dad admired John Wesley's simple theology of money: "Earn all you can, save all you can, give away all you can." Once he regretted not securing a long-term pastoral job before the onset of his neuropathy to maintain a steady income and use his gifts more fully. He kept his funds invested for the long term, never yielding to market fluctuations. When the recession of 2008 dovetailed with the sharp increases for Mom's care, he cut expenses by over half in moving from Parkway Village in Little Rock to a tiny apartment in Mount. Ida., Arkansas. Insisting on generosity, he held to the 10 percent tithe to his church and charities throughout his working life. My parents enjoyed donating to projects like the purchase of two lots in Recife that added to the IBCI church. Dad's close friend Dr. Tom Logue, a weekly breakfast companion, joked with me once during the Little Rock years that "Whatever your dad did with his money, I wish we would have known his secret a longtime ago."[88]

THE TRAVEL HOLY LIFE

Dad was a travel-holic, driven by dreams for the next bike ride, or next road trip, or international travel, which he planned for months. Following him around on a journey was to witness the in-

Dorothy and Glenn enjoyed the mystical Foz do Iguaçu *waterfalls, circa 1970.*

carnation of gratitude. Incredibly grateful for what was before him, be it the haunting fortress of Masada, Israel, the fabled cobble streets of Florence, Italy, the deep Irish green meadows, or the culinary feasts of Minas Gerais, Brazil. Our family took Jim Spann 3,500 kilometers (2,175 miles) in a cozy *Gordini* to the *Foz de Iguaçu*, the epic cascades between Brazil and Argentina. Dad had been dreaming of this trip for many years, having read Eleanor Roosevelt, who, upon viewing the majesty of *Iguaçu*, wrote, "Poor little Niagara Falls, just a waterspout!"

His last publicly declared dream was to travel back and preach at every church he had pastored once more. He accomplished this mission except for First Baptist, Wellington, Texas, choosing instead to go to Recife, Brazil and one last sermon at his beloved *Igreja Batista Central do Ibura*. (IBCI)

Single Until...

It would be an understatement to say Dad missed his life love and partner after she passed into the Light in May of 2010. More than fifty years of faithful marriage had left him with the all sweetness and longing, and no trace of bitterness from Mom's Alzheimer's years. Soon he was ready to date again, or so he thought. He bore the stated and unstated concerns of myself and his sister, Glenna, just like a teenager who knew exactly how to speak to his parents because he knew better than they did. He discovered the highs and lows of elder dating with his own mixture of delight and wonder, occasionally falling into disillusionment with the ordeal. His recourse was prayer, solitude, and healthy doses of brotherhood with men friends like Dwayne Fisher, offering inspiration and advice.

Dad recognized Virginia Atkinson on a TV ad after twenty-five years. He had known Virginia, now a widow, and her husband Charles, who was a pastor at Green Memorial Baptist Church in the Pulaski Baptist Association, when Dad was Director of Missions. Virginia was the star of a commercial for a local senior living facility. He quickly found her phone number in the book and started a whirlwind romance that ended at the altar six months later. They both loved retelling the wedding proposal story: When Dad proposed he only got to the "Will you…" when Virginia blurted out "YES! YES! YES!" From then on, no one dared to stop their octogenarian wedding train.

Double wedding joy! In his advanced neuropathy, Dad courageously left his fiancée for ten days and made his final visit to Brazil in June 2011 to stand beside me for my wedding to Maria Sousa. I then returned the favor in July to be his best man as he tied the Baptist wedding knot to Virginia Atkinson. Dad enjoyed the unexpected gift of having a skilled new daughter-in-law to prepare him in the finest details for his wedding day, including haircut, manicure, pedicure, and tux selection.

The Hickey-Atkinson event even made the local nightly news with the double-walker entry and the drama of both leaning in and maintaining enough balance for a sweet kiss of wedded bliss. For Dad, this marriage was a last act of courage. He embraced the present and found a haven for companionship and mutuality. Virginia would hold court and tell her colorful stories with Dad often adding his own take to their joint Arkansas Baptist folklore. Their relationship was only one-year-and-a-half of joyful conversation, and there was still so much more to say when Dad passed on to the Light in February of 2013.

The Last Visit

In January 2013, Dad was ready to move in with his bride Virginia at the Parkway Village Nursing Home. They were able to talk both families and the Parkway staff into getting adjoining rooms. It was a senior living dream come true! I came back from Brazil for a brief visit to move Dad into his newlywed suite. The time slipped away so quickly. I sat on his bed before my departure as he lay between lucidity and afternoon nap dreamy time.

We frequently joked that our last few years together had reversed our position when our graduating class of the American School of Recife in 1975 said goodbye to their parents in Brazil for stateside universities. A heavy burden of the missionary life is having to say goodbye early and often to your offspring, giving them over to God's care. With wistful hugs, prayers, and tears, we were sent off to *Norte America*, the rite of passage often particularly brutal for these passionate parents. *Saudades* before we even boarded the airplane!

Dad had blessed my return to Brazil to fulfill a life dream of returning to live and work in *Recife*, the beloved land of my youth. This separation was made bearable by Skype and trips back to Arkansas. He endured it with the same grace that had filled his life with so many unforgettable goodbyes and hellos.

"So, do you think you and Maria will move back soon?

"Yes, in a year we plan to, Maria needs to finish school first..."

"OK..."

There was a heavy vapor of sadness coming from under us and filling the room. We couldn't make it go away, so we sat in silence for a long while until I laid my hands on his hands and uttered a prayer. He was breathing so deeply that it scared me. I thought he might be passing on. But then he woke up wide awake, smiled, and said I must be going now, not to miss my flight.

And that was our last goodbye. *SAUDADES!*

Dad and Mom were very attached to their grandchildren, Nathan, Madeleine, and Claire, and the feeling was mutual. They took them in their Airstream to fun destinations and hosted holiday gatherings in their home in Benton, Arkansas. Dad made extraordinary efforts to drive himself to Kansas City to see them all as adults when they could not get away. They all returned the love with a visit to Mom and Dad in her time of illness. Dad was very fond of his talks on the nature of faith and non-faith with Nathan, who reflected:

"I always enjoyed playing guitar for them (Nana and Papa), they would always cry, even for happy songs. I enjoyed those conversations we had about spirituality. He would try to sway me away from atheism…and I would try to sway him toward atheism.

"I remember getting into a debate with him about evolution after he had given me a book by Francis Collins about evolution as intelligent design. I argued it's possible to have evolution and intelligent designs without an intelligent designer. But of course, he would still claim that the intelligent designer existed. I remember another conversation, I think while I was still at Purdue University, where he described a miraculous close call on the highway where he and Nana were not hurt. (A 360-spin with trailer on a Missouri highway on trip to see us in Kansas City). I think when people barely escape from a potentially traumatic event, they often attribute their luck to God looking out for them … and my response was that unlikely events can happen all the time, and not all of them have good outcomes. With seven billion people in the world, chances are high that at least a few people are experiencing some improbable event at any given time, and Papa just happened to be one of those people during his close call on the highway. And if there is a God who has control over things that occur on highways, then it means you have to fault God for all the fatal accidents as well as the near misses.

"I liked the back and forth we had about God or the ways that God would potentially intervene in things. I mean, that was huge part of his life, so I didn't ever expect him to leave that opinion. But he never scolded me or talked down to me for not believing in God. He was always very inquisitive and accepting of my beliefs. He even read that one paper I wrote in college for philosophy class about my lack of belief in God.

"I also remember his preaching, and I thoroughly enjoyed the sermons that he gave. He was a good storyteller, and he would incorporate stories from his own life to show how scripture could relate to day-to-day experiences. I remember one Christmas, Papa was reading from the Bible and Maddie, Claire, and I started laughing, and couldn't stop laughing, not at the Bible verse itself but just laughing, and I think he started laughing himself …I rarely saw him angry. I loved how he went against the grain of the typical grandparent by always being up to date with current technology, even in his old age. It was a pleasure being able to go and help him pick out his computer at Best Buy." (Nathan Hickey, Interview, 2017)

Fear Not!

A legacy of Dad's teaching and preaching was the invitation to *fear not!* The journey from fear to courage to love, or *Metanoia*,[89] another favorite word of his missionary community. The opposite of love is not hate, but fear. He appreciated the care expressed in the goodbye salutation "safe travels," but ultimately that was contrary to the purpose of the missionary journey.

"On this Christmas season of 2010, one of the most relevant verses in all the Christmas story this year is the word of the heavenly messenger to the shepherds in Luke chapter 2, 'Fear Not'! "How can we overcome these fears? Can God help us to face life unafraid? It is interesting to note that one of the words occurring most frequently in the Bible is the word 'fear.' Obviously, this was one of man's greatest problems in that ancient age just as it is today. It is also significant to notice that the command 'fear not' or 'be not afraid' is by far the most frequent command that comes to us from God's word. This would suggest that God wants to deal with the problem of fear in our lives. It was true also in the ministry of Jesus. His most frequent command to his disciples is the command 'fear not, be not afraid!'

"We are living in a time of great fear in our country and around the world. New threats to our security are still looming, North and South Korea are on the brink of War, Iran may soon have a nuclear bomb. We are living in a fearful time. A recent survey of Americans revealed that 80 percent of us see this time is more fearful than the threat of terrorism we felt after nine-eleven. In the United States, suicide was the third leading cause of death among people fifteen to twenty-four years of age. So we come to this Christmas season with a certain fear of what might lie ahead. We struggle with fear and anxiety. Will our retirement nest egg be sufficient? Will we be able to leave anything behind for our children? But in the midst of fear and anxiety, the message God wants to bring us from Bethlehem's manger is a message of hope and joy.

"We are thinking these are the worst of times for our country and our personal lives. But it could be the best of times if these circumstances cause us to look within ourselves and reexamine our fears and our faith. Remember the opposite of fear for a Christian is not courage, but trust in God."[90]

How Big is Your World?

The vocation (calling from God) of missionary is awkward to explain in both secular and religious culture! Dad devoured the writings of Frederick Buechner, who says it well:

"The place God calls you to is the place where your deep gladness and the world's deep hunger meet."[91]

"I grew up in Oden and Mount Ida, in Montgomery County, Arkansas. The world in which I grew up was very small. Until I was thirteen, that world was made up of the thirty-five acre farm we lived on, the Hickey General Mercantile store operated by my grandfather, his two brothers, and my dad. The store, the Oden Baptist Church and the Oden School were all within a mile of each other. When I was thirteen, my dad bought out an old hardware store in Mount Ida, and I thought my world had really expanded when we moved to the big county seat town of Mount Ida.

"What I didn't realize until late was that at nine years of age I had done something that expanded my world a thousand times more than moving from a village of two hundred to a town of two thousand. For you see, at age nine I accepted Jesus as my savior and was baptized in the baptizing hole on the Ouachita river. Little did I realize it at the time, but as a young child I had taken the first step on a lifelong journey that would take me to O.B.C., Southwestern Seminary, the panhandle of Texas, then halfway around the world to the land of Brazil.

"For us, it was God's call to once again stretch the dimensions of our world, pack up our belongings in four gigantic shipping crates, spend a year in Portuguese language study near the city of São Paulo, and then move again to the northeastern coastal city of Recife. We consider those the best years of our lives as we worked with young seminary students who are now serving the Lord all over Brazil and in several countries around the world as missionaries.

"That journey is what we call the Christian life. It is following Jesus wherever he leads us, and it is not a journey just for preachers and missionaries. Anyone who truly becomes a Christian and a follower of Jesus becomes not only a citizen of heaven, but an ambassador for Christ to the whole wide world. So the real question for us today is not how much I shall give. The real question is, How big is your world? What sized world can you fit into your heart? How big of a world can you allow God to love through you?"[92]

Dr. Fred Spann delivered the eulogy at Dr. Glenn Hickey's memorial and was a *Jangadeiro* with him in this adventure on the Recife blue and green ocean waters.

"Anyone who has traveled to the northeast Brazilian coast recognizes the crude fishing crafts called *Jangadas*. Consisting of eight to ten balsa logs lashed together, a triangular sail and a rustic wooden bench, fisherman venture out as far as the continental shelf (about ten to twelve miles) to bring back seafood—lobster, shrimp, oyster, and a variety of fish for their family and to sell at markets. They have become a trademark of cities on the warm tropical Atlantic Coast.

"Early in our missionary career, Wade Smith, Glenn Hickey, Norton Lages, and I decided to try out fishing from the *Jangada*. Fortunately, we located someone who would rent his boat, so we could bring a fine catch back to our families at the mission vacation house on the Piedade beach south of Boa Viajem. Early in the morning we set out; we had some fishing lines, adequate bait (we thought), and began to make our way out beyond the reefs, hoping the waves would favor journeying in the direction of where the fishermen indicated we would certainly make a good catch. Norton, a Brazilian seminary student, was who we were depending on for our success since he was raised on the Amazon in equatorial Brazil.

"The *Jangada* was really quite safe, we assumed, since it is constructed from lightweight balsa wood and can't sink, and we had an anchor to use for stability. Anyway, we zig-zagged out to 'the spot.' The ocean was much rougher than we anticipated. The problem was the ceaseless, unrelenting waves building to ever larger swells. We had taken no precautionary measures for motion sickness. We all began to sense a sickly numbness. Fishing had lost its charm. We all felt like regurgitating. We were simply terribly seasick.

"So, we attempted to make our way back to shore. Bettye saw us coming, called the kids, and everyone, including several Brazilians gathered, expecting a fine fish fry for dinner. As we were plodding to-

The legendary Jangadeiros: Wade Smith, Norton Lages, Glenn Hickey and Fred Spann.

ward the beach, suddenly a large wave caught us sideways and the *Jangada* capsized. You talk about confusion! All types of gear-tackle boxes, ropes, anchor, sail, paddles—you name it, almost everything to the bottom of the sea. Three of us managed to get on the upside-down boat, but Glenn was underneath tangled in the mess of ropes. Finally, he appeared, safe!

"We were four discouraged, sea-sick, amateur fishermen and we looked like four drowned sea rats just trying to get back to land. It was a sad moment as we approached our families. They were expecting hero dads. We, just hoping to somehow make it to shore! And it didn't help any when, after realizing we were all safe, they couldn't contain themselves and were bent over in uncontrollable laughter! Needless to say, we didn't get much sympathy." (Dr. Fred Spann, Memoirs)

We are eternally grateful that Dad untangled himself! Glenn, Dorothy, and their colleagues were *Jangadeiros*. They were on a high adventure into the joy of the Gospel as they offered their lives to others. Their mysticism was a feet-on-the-ground quest to fish for men and women who might touch, hear, and see the transcendent through them, thus opening themselves to join their struggle toward the Christian light way. It was an adventure that none would trade for the world.

Epilogue

This Pandemic will end and how will we respond to the opportunity for a new beginning? What new dreams will arise and what fears must be overcome with love to reach them? A new world will be created by dreamers and dream makers. The boundaries and old ways will need courageous and compassionate travelers to cross the planet or cross the street in the name of love. We have been passed a torch of hope and joy by those we lost to carry on more faithing in the despair, more vision than our own tribal good, and more illumination in the darkness.

Illuminated suggestions:

Glenn and Dorothy Hickey funded the first 2 years of *Transformational Journeys*. The mission continues: "To introduce individuals to experiences that can inspire compassion, develop understanding, and promote generosity through mutual service with people of other cultures." Send a message to our Director Candace Kaster to check out the upcoming trips (www.tjourneys.org and change-ofscenery-changeofheart.blogspot.com).

The Bucket Ministry—Layne and Betty Sparks (Dad's cousin from the Gang of Four) daughter Kristi Brown and their granddaughter Karen Brown are extending the mission legacy of our family. These cousins lead international volunteer trips with the Bucket Ministry, "a passionate group of ordinary people from many different churches, different countries and many different walks of life. The mission of our ministry is sharing the Love of God through the gift of clean, safe drinking water (thebucketministry.org).

Endnotes

1 "Converted," The English word "conversion" is associated with the Hebrew word *shuv*, which means to turn back or return, and the Greek words *epistrepho* and *metanoeo*, both of which indicate to turn towards God. The key term in the New Testament is the latter, together with its noun form *metanoia*. This term signifies not simply a change of mind (as in classical Greek) but a change of heart. *Christianity Today* Archives, Donald Bloesch, May 24th, 1968.

2 "On Keeping Our Dreams Alive," Glenn Hickey collection, Special collections, Box 1, O.B.U. Archives.

3 "The Appearing of the Son of Man," Glenn Hickey collection, Special collections, Box 1, O.B.U. Archives.

4 "When God Calls," Glenn Hickey collection, Special collections, Box 1, O.B.U. Archives.

5 "What a friend we have in Jesus," Glenn Hickey collection, Special collections, Box 1, O.B.U. Archives.

6 "What a friend we have in Jesus," Glenn Hickey collection, Special collections, Box 1, O.B.U. Archives.

7 Zahle Elms Journals, Glenn Hickey collection, Special collections, Box 1, O.B.U. Archives.

8 Ouachita Baptist College became Ouachita Baptist University in 1965.

9 Merriam Webster Online Dictionary, Incorporated, 2020 <Merriam-Webster.com>, April 22, 2020.

10 Zahle Elms Journals, Glenn Hickey collection, Special collections, Box 1, O.B.U. Archives.

11 Zahle Elms Journals, Glenn Hickey collection, Special collections, Box 1, O.B.U. Archives. (Musical highlights of the Ouachita

Quartet, Dorothy and Glenn Hickey's duets, and Dorothy's solos are available in the O.B.U. Archives, Glenn Hickey collection, Special collections, O.B.U. Archives.)

12 "When God Calls," Glenn Hickey collection, Special collections, Box 1, O.B.U. Archives.

13 "Power to Walk Through the Storms of Life," Mark 6:46-50; Matthew 14:28-33, Glenn Hickey collection, Special collections, Box 1, O.B.U. Archives.

14 "The Divine Regime: Brazilian Baptists Between Autonomy and Centralization (1881–1935)." ALVES, Pedro Henrique G. T., Dissertation (Pgs 55-60), Fundação Getulio Vargas, Rio de Janeiro, 2019.

15 "Confronting Christ who is Always There," Glenn Hickey collection, Special collections, Box 1, O.B.U. Archives.

16 "Putting Christ First," Glenn Hickey collection, Special collections, Box 1, O.B.U. Archives.

17 *Two Countries, Two Families, One God*, Ruth Worthington Carter, "WestBow Press, 2013.

18 "Surprised by Hell," Calvary Sermons 7/6/80 (AM) CDs,Glenn Hickey collection, Special collections, O.B.U. Archives.

19 Zahle Elms Journals, Glenn Hickey collection, Special collections, Box 1, O.B.U. Archives.

20 *Daring Greatly: How the Courage to Be Vulnerable Transforms the Way We Live, Love, Parent, and Lead*, Dr. Brené Brown, Avery Publishing, 2012.

21 "Lord Open Our Eyes," Calvary Sermons 2/22/81 (PM) CDs Glenn Hickey collection, Special collections, O.B.U. Archives.

22 "The Gold of the Gospel or the Gospel of Gold," Calvary Sermons, Glenn Hickey collection, Special collections, CDs, O.B.U. Archives.

23 "The Lost Son," Calvary sermons, Glenn Hickey collection, Special collections, CDs, O.B.U. Archives.

24 Sermon title unknown, Glenn Hickey collection, Special collections, Box 1, O.B.U. Archives.

25 Founded by the Author, *Transformational Journeys* is a volunteer vacation organization whose mission continues to thrive host-

ing groups in Guatemala: "To introduce individuals to experiences that can inspire compassion, develop understanding, and promote generosity through mutual service with people of other cultures." Glenn and Dorothy Hickey generously funded the first 2 years of Transformational Journeys. Their mission legacy lives on where current Director Candace Kaster hosts a menu of reverse mission trips every year. (A reverse mission trip is when those who go to serve are surprised by the joy in those they serve) https://www.facebook.com/transformational.journeys/.

26 "Religion and Race," The United Methodist Church, Dr. Arthuree Wright, February 2020, <http://www.gcorr.org/25-traits-of-the-beloved-community>, February 26, 2020.

27 Bill Ichter, New Book of Memoirs, Part 1.

28 "What I Want Most for Christmas," Calvary Sermons 12/13/81 (PM) CDs, Glenn Hickey collection, Special collections, O.B.U. Archives.

29 *The Freud/Jung Letters*, William MacGuire, 1974.

30 "Guests Billy Simmons and the Bethlehem Baptist Choir," Calvary CDs, Glenn Hickey collection, Special collections, O.B.U. Archives.

31 *Woman in the World of Jesus*, Frank and Evelyn Stagg, 1978, Westminster Press.

32 "Jimmy Carter Renounces Southern Baptist Convention," Belief net, October 20, 2000 <http://beliefnet.com/story/47/story_4798_1.html> May 15th, 2019.

33 Habakkuk, Chapter 2:2-4, N.I.V.
"Then the Lord replied: "Write down the revelation, and make it plain on tablet, so that a herald may run with it. For the revelation awaits an appointed time, it speaks of the end, and will not prove false. Though it linger, wait for it, it will certainly come, and will not delay. "See, the enemy is puffed up; his desires are not upright, but the righteous person will live by his faithfulness."

34 Matthew 28, 16-20 (NIV)
"Then the eleven disciples went to Galilee, to the mountain where Jesus had told them to go. When they saw him, they worshiped him; but some doubted. Then Jesus came to them and said, "All authority in heaven and on earth has been given to me. Therefore, go and make disciples of all nations, baptizing them in the name of the Father and of the Son and

of the Holy Spirit, and teaching them to obey everything I have commanded you, and surely I am with you always, to the very end of the age."

35 "Pulaski Baptist Association Annual Meeting Address," 1985, Glenn Hickey collection, Special collections, Box 1, O.B.U. Archives.

36 "Bernie Self Oral History Series," Glenn Hickey collection, Special collections, O.B.U. Archives.

37 Csikszentmihalyi, M. *Flow: The Psychology of Optimal Experience*, Harper and Row. 1990.

38 "Christianity according to the Good Samaritan," Biblical World, PG 147, March,1916, Glenn Hickey collection, Special collections, O.B.U. Archives.

39 "The Danger of Emptiness," Calvary Sermons, 7/27/80 (PM)CDs, Glenn Hickey collection, Special collections, O.B.U. Archives.

40 "Failure is Never Fatal," Matthew 26:31-35;69-75, 6/6/04 Glenn Hickey collection, Special collections, Box 1, O.B.U. Archives.

41 "God has Spoken, Therefore," (Hebrews 1,2) Trinity Baptist Church, Little Rock, 10/21/01 Glenn Hickey collection, Special collections, Box 1, O.B.U. Archives.

42 Sermon title unknown, Glenn Hickey collection, Special collections, Box 1, O.B.U. Archives.

43 "What Did You Say," Calvary Sermons, 5/11/80 (PM) CDs, Glenn Hickey collection, Special collections, CDs, O.B.U. Archives.

44 Sermon title unknown, Glenn Hickey collection, Special collections, Box 1, O.B.U. Archives.

45 "The Good Seed and the Bad," Calvary sermons, 7/20/80 (AM) CDs, Matt. 13: 24-30 Glenn Hickey collection, Special collections, O.B.U. Archives.

46 "The Cost of Forgiveness," Calvary Sermons, 7/27/80 (AM), CDs, Glenn Hickey collection, Special collections, O.B.U. Archives.

47 "Waking Up Time," Romans 13:11-14, Calvary Sermons, 4/27/80 CDs Glenn Hickey collection, Special collections, O.B.U. Archives.

48 "Gods Design for Motherhood," 5/11/80 (AM) Glenn Hickey collection, Special collections, CDs, O.B.U. Archives.

49 "Thyatira: Keeping at it Till Christ Comes," Calvary Sermons, 11/2/80, (PM), CDs, Glenn Hickey collection, Special collections, O.B.U. Archives.

50 "The Destructive Power of Evil," Calvary Sermons, Glenn Hickey collection, Special collections, O.B.U. Archives.

51 "God's final work to man" Calvary Sermons, 2/8/81 (PM), CDs, Rev.22; Source: Chuck Wagner's radio program, "Night Watch" Glenn Hickey collection, Special collections, O.B.U. Archives.

52 "Beyond History," Calvary Sermons, 11/16/80 (AM) CDs, Rev.4:1-11 Glenn Hickey collection, Special collections, O.B.U. Archives.

53 Parkway Village Friday Bible Study, "James: Plain Talk About the Christian Life," Glenn Hickey collection, Special collections, Box 1, O.B.U. Archives.

54 "On Eagles' Wings, the God-directed life," Isaiah 40:30-31 Glenn Hickey collection, Special collections, Box 1, O.B.U. Archives.

55 "David, A Man after Gods Own Heart," Calvary Sermons 6/7/81 (AM), CDs Acts 13:22 Glenn Hickey collection, Special collections, CDs, O.B.U. Archives.

56 Dr L. Michael White is a leading scholar, author, archeologist and a Professor of Religious Studies at the University of Texas, Austin. He dives deeply into why the synoptic gospels differ so dramatically from the later written Gospel of John. He points out that even the early church recognizes this. "Already by the year 200, John's gospel was called the spiritual gospel precisely because it told the story of Jesus in symbolic ways that differ sharply at times from the other three. For example, Jesus dies on a different day in John's gospel than in Matthew, Mark and Luke.... Whereas in the three synoptic gospels Jesus eats a Passover meal before he dies, in John's gospel he doesn't.... One must look at it and say, why is this story so different?" (*Scripting Jesus: The Gospels in Rewrite*, L. Michael White, Harper Collins, 2010)

For those hungry for more on how the Bible was inspired and written, I strongly recommend his work *From Jesus to Christianity: How Four Generations of Visionaries and Storytellers Created the New Testament and Christian Faith*. (L. Michael White, Harper One, 2004)

57 *Mysterium tremendum*—"The feeling of it may at times come sweeping like a gentle tide pervading the mind with a tranquil mood of deepest worship. It may pass over into a more set and lasting attitude of the soul, continuing, as it were, thrillingly vibrant and resonant, until at

last it dies away and the soul resumes its 'profane,' non-religious mood of everyday experience" (Rudolf Otto, German Theologian and Philosopher, and Historian, *The Idea of the Holy*, 1923).

58 *From Jesus to Christianity: How Four Generations of Visionaries & Storytellers Created the New Testament and Christian Faith*, L. Michael White, Harper One, 2004.

59 "How God Makes Us Right," Calvary Sermons, 3/7/82, (AM) CDs, Romans 3:21-31, Glenn Hickey collection, Special collections, CDs, O.B.U. Archives.

60 "Like a Lamb Who Needs a Shepherd," Calvary Sermons, CDs, Psalm 23, Glenn Hickey collection, Special collections, O.B.U. Archives.

61 "God's Word for the World," Calvary Sermons, CDs, Rev 10, Glenn Hickey collection, Special collections, O.B.U. Archives.

62 "Don't Let Anything Destroy Your Dream," Calvary Sermons, 1/3/82, (AM), CDs, Glenn Hickey collection, Special collections, O.B.U. Archives.

63 "Don't Let Anything Destroy Your Dream," Calvary Sermons, 1/3/82, (AM), CDs, Glenn Hickey collection, Special collections, O.B.U. Archives.

64 Sermon title unknown, Luke 9:59-62 and 14:25-26, Glenn Hickey collection, Special collections, Box 1, O.B.U. Archives.

65 "The Mystery of Iniquity," Calvary Sermons, Rev 13-14, Glenn Hickey collection, Special collections, CDs, O.B.U. Archives.

66 "The Curse of Uselessness," CDs, Calvary Sermons, Mark 11: 12-20, Glenn Hickey collection, Special collections, O.B.U. Archives.

67 "Abraham, God's Promise, and Man's Response," Calvary Sermons, Romans 4:14-25, Glenn Hickey collection, Special collections, Box 1, O.B.U. Archives.

68 "We Are the Life Givers," John Chapter 10:10, 20:19-23,30-31, Glenn Hickey collection, Special collections, Box 1, O.B.U. Archives. The story of "The Star Thrower" is from *The Unexpected Universe* by Loren Eiseley, Harcourt, Brace and World, 1969.

69 "Gods Final Work to Man," Calvary Sermons, CDs, Rev. 22, Glenn Hickey collection, Special collections, O.B.U. Archives.

70 "The Fire and the Wind," Glenn Hickey collection, Special collections, Box 1, O.B.U. Archives.

71 "Everyone Needs Friends," Mark 2:1-12, Glenn Hickey collection, Special collections, Box 1, O.B.U. Archives. The accuracy of when and where the Jackie Robinson story took place is not established. Pewee Reese was interviewed by Dave Kindred in 1997: "Just don't make me out to be a hero," Reese said. "It took no courage to do what I did. Jackie had the courage. If it had been me, a white man, trying to be the only one in the black leagues, I couldn't have done it. What he had to endure, the criticism, the catcalls — I wouldn't have had the courage."

72 "The Cost of Forgiveness," Matthew 18:23-25, Glenn Hickey collection, Special collections, Box 1, O.B.U. Archives.

73 "Bruised but Blessed," Genesis 28: 10-17, 2nd Corinthians, 12:7-10, Glenn Hickey collection, Special collections, Box 1, O.B.U. Archives, *The Wounded Healer*, Henri Nouwen, 1979, The Crown Publishing Group.

74 *Future Shock*, Alvin Toffler, Random House, 1970.

75 "Christ in the Midst of His Churches," Calvary Sermons, 10/26/80, (AM) CDs, Rev. 1:9-20, Glenn Hickey collection, Special collections, O.B.U. Archives.

76 Sermon title unknown, Calvary Sermons 1/25/81 (AM), Glenn Hickey collection, Special collections, CDs, O.B.U. Archives.

77 "The Christ who is Always There," Calvary Sermons 4/19/81, Glenn Hickey collection, Special collections, Box 1, O.B.U. Archives.

78 "The Great Surprise," Calvary Sermons, 8/10/80 (AM), CDs Matthew 25:31-46, Glenn Hickey collection, Special collections, O.B.U. Archives.

79 "A Church for the Third Millennium," Glenn Hickey collection, Special collections, Box 1, O.B.U. Archives.

80 "Survival or Revival," Calvary Sermons 5/24/18 (AM) CDs, 2 Peter 3: 10-14, Glenn Hickey collection, Special collections, Box 1, O.B.U. Archives.

81 Sermon title unknown, Glenn Hickey collection, Special collections, Box 1, O.B.U. Archives.

82 "How to Live a Joyful Life," Calvary Sermons, Source: Dr Rex Horne Jr., Philippians 1:1-25 Glenn Hickey collection, Special collections, Box 1, O.B.U. Archives.

83 "Standing Firm in Our Freedom," Gal. 5:1, Glenn Hickey collection, Special collections, Box 1, O.B.U. Archives.

84 "Ready for Christ's Return," Calvary Sermons, 7/6/80, (PM) CDs, Matthew 25: 1-13, Glenn Hickey collection, Special collections, O.B.U. Archives.

85 Temporal Power: "Of or relating to time as opposed to eternity; of or relating to earthly life; lay or secular rather than clerical or sacred" Merriam-Webster.com. 2020. https://www.merriam-webster.com January 25, 2020.

86 *His Political Philosophy and Its Application to Our Age as Expressed in His Writings, Reinhold Niebuhr on Politics*, Edited by Harry Davis and Robert Good, 1960.

87 *Why Religion.* Elaine Pagels, HarperCollins, 2018, pgs. 1-2.

88 Dr. Tom Logue, State Director of Baptist Student Union of Arkansas from 1955-1987. Dr. Logue served as founding coordinator of the Cooperative Baptist Fellowship of Arkansas from 1991–2005. Tom was key in the author's decision to serve in Campus Ministry for 20 years.

89 *Metanoia*—Second language learning missionary biblical exegetes are fond of this Greek word, because the pronunciation is almost the same in English, Portuguese, Spanish and French.

90 Sermon title unknown, Luke 2 :8-14, Glenn Hickey collection, Special collections, Box 1, O.B.U. Archives.

91 *Wishful Thinking: A Theological ABC*, Frederick Buechner, Harper One, 1973.

92 "A Men's Breakfast Meditation, First Baptist Benton," Glenn Hickey collection, Special collections, Box 1, O.B.U. Archives.

Acknowledgments

Obrigado is thank you in Portuguese. It means I am obligated to you for your kindness.

Dr. Bob Boury, who knew my father well, edited the first draft with a passion for Dr. Glenn Hickey's legacy and my dream of sharing it.

The Artist Couple—Sarah Mack is my father's grandniece, the granddaughter of Uncle Bob and Glenna Lybrand. It was another priceless gift on this book writing journey to have her imagine and illustrate my Parent's lives so accurately. Her partner Topher Mack provided targeted direction and encouragement.

Dr. Ray Granade donated many hours of his time and expertise in the editing of this work. I am honored for his presence to its pages.

The kindness and generosity of eight Uncles and Aunts nurtured this book along until adulthood much like they nurtured my life from childhood into the big person world:

Missionaries Aunt Glenda and Uncle Dave Miller—A foundational couple in our missionary community, and part of our extended family, helping us MKs to find our feet and wings along the way. They provided treasured insight into my parents' aspirations and struggles from the Brazil years to their last days.

Missionaries Aunt Bettye and Uncle Fred Spann—Brazil mission colleagues and fellow Arkansans who served side by side with my parents almost every day of their Recife years. Uncle Fred was incredibly generous in sharing his own memoirs. Aunt Bettye, my mother's best friend on the mission field, delighted in sharing the human stories of "what really happened that time was…"

My Uncle Bob and Aunt Glenna Lybrand—They both were steady guides in the growth of this narrative, and the difference makers in the watch-care for my parents during their elder years.

My father's cousin Betty Sparks and her husband, Layne Sparks, his first best friend, who retold the early stories of Dad's life with passion and imagination.

Missionary Uncle Steve Long, who lived in the "Hickey House" after my parents retired from Brazil and became close to them on subsequent visits. His reflection on this work was a treasure.

Missionary Aunt Barbara Martin, who knew my parents well during the Brazil years, took time from her Christmas break and offered suggestions for the text to become kinder to the reader.

My Brazil M.K. "cousins" Joy Eastridge, R.N. and a published author herself, and Dr. James Spann of N.A.S.A., who knew my parents as Uncle Glenn and Aunt Dorothy, both went over and above the call by reading cover to cover in the midst of heavy schedules, and then offering detailed advice and reviews.

Appreciation for the enduring patience of Dr. Wendy Richter, O.B.U. Professor and Archivist, and Dr. Lisa Speer, O.B.U. Associate Professor and Archivist, who at separate times during the gestation of this work were inspirational in presence to their calling.

Obrigado de coraçaõ!

Thanks from my heart!

About the Author

After the quirky blessing of being formed in a family who served creatively as Southern Baptist missionaries in Brazil, Daniel Hickey has had a funky-fun life with four careers that were on the edge of adventure and sometimes falling right off. He learned early that living between cultures was a lifegiving riot. Following the family lead, after a higher education involving a B.A. in History (Ouachita Baptist University and University of Arkansas) and a Masters of Divinity (Midwestern Baptist Theological Seminary), he settled into 20 years of Campus Ministry, most of these at William Jewell College in Liberty, MO. This led to the fortuitous path of founding *Transformational Journeys*, a Volunteer  Mission Travel Company based in Kansas City. "T.J." continues to thrive under Director Candace Kaster, hosting trips to Guatemala.

His passion for Intercultural Education led to co-founding Brasil cultura, a Brazilian Cultural presentation company where he enjoyed creating culture shock for Kansas, Missouri and Arkansas audiences with real *Samba* and *Capoeira*. After a four-year immersion as a Spanish teacher in Arkansas and English teacher in Brazil, he finally made a lifelong passion into a career:

Spanish/English and Portuguese/English language interpretation in culturally diverse central Arkansas.

Daniel is blessed to be married to Maria Sousa, a native Brazilian and naturalized American who has inspired his current journey as an author. They live in Little Rock with their dog Zeus, and love their international community in the Natural State! They rejoice in being a part of St Michael's Episcopal community in Little Rock, where "In the spirit of St. Michael, we seek to vanquish the modern-day dragons of poverty, disease and intolerance."

CPSIA information can be obtained
at www.ICGtesting.com
Printed in the USA
LVHW052024120820
662996LV00005B/362

9 781733 796446